The Lake Louise Commission

The Sacred Family

American Lutheran Publicity Bureau
Delhi, New York

Two previous books authorized
by Ascension Lutheran Church:

The Banff Commission (2008)
and
The Jasper Commission (2009)

are also available at

www.alpb.org

The cover image is by Gustave Koenig as it appeared in
The Small Catechism of Dr. Martin Luther with 75 Illustrations,
5th ed. (Reading, PA: Pilgrim Book Store, 1905).

2011 © ALPB Books

ISBN 1-892921-19-7

American Lutheran Publicity Bureau
PO Box 327
Delhi, NY 13753

The Lake Louise Commission: The Sacred Family (Delhi, NY:
American Lutheran Publicity Bureau, 2011), 124 pp.

Contents

Preface

K. Glen Johnson

Casiodoro de Reina wrote the following in his *Ecclesium Christi*:

No one who has studied the matter will deny that in the course of its entire history the fortunes of the Church on earth have been determined in such a way that its preservation from harm or its downfall have depended exclusively on its pastors and bishops. From the foundation of the world the Church has always maintained its strength and flourished when these have faithfully persevered in their mission with fortitude. And the contrary is also true, that things could not have gone any worse for the Church than when its pastors and bishops have allowed themselves to be corrupted by Satan and have been in one way or another ousted from their positions. So, to achieve his ends as quickly as possible, the devil's chief concern is to stalk pious pastors and their ministries tirelessly, directing all the might of his vile nature solely to corrupting them, since their fall will of necessity bring in its train the collapse of the Church.[1]

---

1. *For All the Saints: A Prayer Book For and By the Church*, Vol. 1. (Delhi: American Lutheran Publicity Bureau, 1994), 833. Originally published in 1573.

The teaching, or lack thereof, which is leading to the collapse of the Church in our day, is centered in the first order of creation, the sacred family, male and female, husband and wife, father and mother. The clearly defined order that declares we were created and formed in the image of God is being summarily dismissed and replaced with new and different versions of human identities.

While the current redefining of the first order of creation may seem strange at first glance, it ought not to surprise us at all. Have we not, and do we not continue to define and redefine the very nature of God?

The teaching of the two natures of Christ received its most authoritative formulation at the Council of Chalcedon. Identifying three states in the history of the person of Christ, Hilary spoke of Jesus being only divine before his incarnation, of being both divine and human from his conception to his death, and still being completely man and completely God in his exaltation.

Is it not amazing to consider that God has so loved and honoured his human children that even now the one perfect man remains in union with God?

Because God so loved and honoured the first order of creation it becomes all the more imperative that we also so respect and love and honour what God has created. If we wish to be faithful as pastors and bishops and parents and teachers we can do no more and no less than teach what God and his Spirit through the Scriptures and the Tradition of the Church Catholic have taught. The contributors to this publication have faithfully, boldly and clearly done precisely that.

If we follow their lead, in the strength of the Holy Spirit, the current attack can be repelled and the Church and our society renewed. For this we pray without ceasing.

The Lake Louise Commission Mandate

Ascension Lutheran of Calgary, Alberta, has authorized Pastor K. Glen Johnson to establish an international ecumenical commission to address the debacle and disaster that has overtaken two Lutheran Churches in North America. The Evangelical Lutheran Church in America at its 2009 convention did approve the blessing of same sex unions and the ordination of those living in such relationships. The Evangelical Lutheran Church in Canada will follow the lead of the ELCA in 2011. It was and it will be done.

The Banff and Jasper Commissions were asked to give a truly scriptural, confessional, ecumenical and prophetic word to pastors and congregations who wished to remain faithful in their life and proclamation, as well as to minister effectively to every community, including those with orientations other than heterosexual. The participants spoke the truth with boldness and with clarity.

God's judgement always prevails when the shepherds of the church lead their people astray. The call to repent and to hearken to the Word of the Lord is always on the table for all to see and hear. That judgement is now touching every one of us. For Lutherans, especially in this time of tumult, it may indeed be profitable to hearken to the voice of Martin Luther as he speaks to us through the centuries about the nurture of the family and the people of God. He, too, was utterly appalled by the "wretched deprivation" that he encountered in his parish visitation. The small and large catechisms reflect his judgement and his understanding of what God was saying to his generation of families, pastors and bishops. If Luther were present among us now and saw the affirmed blessing of same sex relationships, the silent blessing of many other forms of sexual license, the unthinkable abortion holocaust, and the dissolution of families in our society, he would not hesitate to speak as boldly as ever to our pastors and bishops and families.

The members of the Lake Louise Commission are being called upon to speak to our time and to allow brother Martin to also speak God's Word through the commission presentations, the official title being:

The Lake Louise Commission

A 21ST CENTURY ADDENDUM
TO LUTHER'S CATECHISMS

concerning:

THE FIRST ORDER OF GOD'S CREATION
– THE SACRED FAMILY

MALE AND FEMALE – HUSBAND AND WIFE

SET APART TO BE CO-CREATORS WITH GOD

CALLED TO BE PRIESTS AND BISHOPS
AND MODELS OF THE GODLY LIFE

AND STEWARDS OF CREATION AND
ALL THINGS LIVING INCLUDING
THE SACRALITY OF LIFE IN UTERO!

The Nature of Marriage

J. Larry Yoder

An Inheritance of Privilege

In regard to both marriage and heritage, I stand in a legacy of continuity. The Yoders of North Carolina's Lincoln County stem from Mennonite immigrant Konrad Jotter, who came to the area in the 1750s as a young unmarried man from Switzerland via the Palatine. In the colony he married, in 1763, a young woman of the Reformed faith, Christina Klein, daughter of a Catawba County pioneer. Christina died in 1772. Konrad then married a Miss Seitz in 1773; she passed away a year later. His final marriage was to Katarina Huffman, herself a German immigrant, in 1775; Katarina survived him when he died in 1790. Each of his three marriages ended by the death of one of the partners. Konrad and his family worshipped in a "union" church – where Reformed and Lutheran congregations occupied the same building, attending alternately Reformed and Lutheran services. (The two congregations – Zion Lutheran and Bethel UCC – now occupy separate buildings, but are in sight of each other in southern Catawba County.)

The second generation (David) walked across the aisle to Lutheran affiliation. David (1770-1864) married Elizabeth Reib

(Reep), who died in 1846, on Reformation Day. David did not remarry. He and Elizabeth were members of Grace Union Church, which was served by his grandson Robert Anderson Yoder in the late 1890s, and presently, as Grace Evangelical Lutheran Church, by his great-great-great grandson Jacob Larry Yoder.

The third generation (Solomon and Sarah Seagle Yoder) bought the farm in Lincoln County in 1832—the year of their marriage—building near the spring a log cabin, complete with loft. Solomon Yoder died in 1854, and Sarah twenty years later, not having remarried.

Their son William married Sarah Mosteller Yoder, and they bought out his brothers and sisters to settle on the family farm. William disassembled the log cabin and moved it up the hill to use as a granary, nearby the two-story frame farmhouse he built for Sarah. The "old log granary" yet stands, still sturdy and still in use. William died in 1900; Sarah did not remarry.

Their son Luther Arthur Yoder married Etta Clare Warlick on November 11, 1905. Luther died in July of 1964, and Clare a year later in May, the two having been married fifty-nine years, and Luther having worked the family farm for his entire working life.

On the Miller side, my mother Mary Katheryn was the second child born to Edward Leondo Miller and Mary Poovey Miller, who were married in 1906. Granddaddy Ed passed away in May of 1960, and Grandmother Mary died in the spring of 1972. They were together as a married couple for fifty-four years.

Jacob Ralph Yoder and Mary Katheryn Miller Yoder were married on the 20th of June 1935. I was born in May of 1943, my brother Wayne in December of 1944, and my sister Mary in July of 1949. Ralph and Mary Katheryn celebrated their 50th anniversary in 1985. Ralph died in 1989 and Mary Katheryn on Good Friday of 2007, several months in advance of her 96th birthday.

As to my wife Marianne Howard Yoder: Woodrow Wilson Howard and Elizabeth Gibson Howard were married on January 15, 1938. Wilson died in October of 2006, having been married to Elizabeth for 68 years and change. Elizabeth, herself now 93, still lives in West Columbia, South Carolina.

Marianne Howard and I met the first day she was a student at Lenoir-Rhyne, Sunday the 8th of September, 1963, fell in love virtually instantly, talked less than a month later (October 4, her 18th birthday) about marriage, and married after she graduated in three years, on 19 June, 1966, 45 years ago this June. Marianne and I have three sons: Nathan Howard Yoder, who is married to Rebecca Cotton Yoder; Joshua Howard Yoder, who is married to Jennifer Hoffman Yoder; and David Howard Yoder, who is married to Kristin Kolster Yoder. David and Krissy have two daughters, Marianne Kolster Yoder and Caroline Kolster Yoder.

Marianne and I live on the Yoder family farm, the one bought in 1832, in the house that William and Sarah built, Luther and Clare expanded, and Ralph and Mary Katheryn remodeled. Marianne and I have restored and, again, expanded the farmhouse…for the purpose of family gatherings.

In all those marriages, save the last, which yet flourishes, the cause of separation was the death of one of the spouses. The most recent have all endured 50 or more years. And none, to my knowledge, was marred or imperiled by incidents, much less episodes, of what commonly is referred to as "infidelity." There was no information concerning that, and no innuendo or rumor. Just "keep yourself only unto him/her, so long as you both shall live."

Thus, as to marriage, I write from a position privileged by the absence of factors that have eroded both the nature and the structure of marriage in North America in the last fifty years.

The Foundations of Family

As to family, Marianne and I discerned in San Diego, serving first as intern and then as associate pastor at Christ Lutheran Church in Pacific Beach, that most of the young people—children and teenagers—hardly knew either set of grandparents, so far removed was nearly every family from its Midwestern or Northeastern roots. So we determined that we would make a sincere effort to raise our family, should we have children, near at least one set of grandparents (i.e., in the Columbia or in the Hickory/Lincolnton area). That meant that, after graduate school, I should seek a call either to Lutheran Theological Southern Seminary or to Lenoir-Rhyne. The place turned out to be Lenoir-Rhyne.

"Train up a child in the way he should go and when he is old he will not depart from it" (Proverbs 22:6). For us that included involvement of both Mother and Dad. Together we shepherded the boys through parochial school at St. Stephen's Lutheran, active involvement at St. Andrew's as members, Boy Scout Troop at First Methodist, music lessons, plays and concerts at Lenoir-Rhyne, working in the garden at the farm, sports according to inclination, letting each boy gravitate to his interests, making sure that his interests consisted of what is good, in principle, living more modestly as Marianne deferred full-time work so as to be the more involved with the boys, she worked part-time as a buyer for her father's department store, and was an intellectual inspiration to her sons when she went back to school to study philosophy. Throughout the years, Marianne took Nathan, Joshua, and David to events in which their Dad had leadership responsibilities as pastor or professor, and, when Marianne was in graduate school, Dad became "Mr. Mom." We stressed "Team Yoder"—respect and encouragement for each other—and "doing one's best" within the context of loving God.

Our goals included the centrality of our Christian faith, devotion to family and concern for neighbor, education toward the good, and integrity instilled through example. As to the last of those: be the same person at home that you are in public. No hypocrisy, no pretense.

Observations and Testimony from Lenoir-Rhyne Students regarding Marriage

The experience of my family is of one sort, as outlined above. The experience of my students runs more often in the direction of the greater culture, as the patterns have emerged over the past three-quarters of a century. There follow excerpts from the essays of a few, among students who submitted papers for "extra credit" as an assignment.[1]

Kimberly – Religion 400 – The Christian Perspective – Capstone Course

I believe that there are people out there that can (be) a marriage together, but I believe that there are even more people out there who lie. When it comes to being faithful to a spouse, I have never been unfaithful, and I have stayed committed even when it hurt my children and me. With this, yes, I have been married three times since I was 18. I gave my first husband two children and my second husband one, and my current husband and I do not want children.

---

1. I put the question about the state of marriage and family in the United States to Lenoir-Rhyne students, those taking courses with me this semester. Some are freshmen, enrolled in the introductory course (REL 100), "The Christian Faith," which examines the "nature of faith;" "what informs Christians," as an introduction to Biblical studies, and "what Christians believe," a review of doctrine central to the faith. Other respondents are enrolled in REL 400, "The Christian Perspective," a "capstone" course for seniors (some enrolled are juniors) which addresses issues of Christianity and Culture, and Christian Ethics.

My first husband cheated on me and fathered another child with another woman, while we were married. Shortly after, we were divorced. I was only 23. I then remarried when I was 26 and by the time I was 30, I found out that my husband was having an affair with his first wife. We then divorced within a year and a half. I then remarried again, for the third time, when I was 34. I wish that I could go back, do it all over again, and make my life right. Commitment should not be this darn hard. I believe that it is a parent's responsibility to help their children understand more about commitment and what it takes to make it work. I do believe that marriage is sacred, but now I believe that people should wait and let God guide their way to find the right person for them. I am still not happy at where I am in life with regards to marriage, but I am one hundred percent committed to my husband. I just hope that he is the same.

As to the phenomenon of divorce, I wish that I could give a better example of this one, but I believe I am a part of the creation of divorce. My parents were married three times apiece. My mom is still married to the third husband, and, of course, my dad has been divorced from his third wife for about 14 years. My dad's dad was divorced once, but he remarried in the 70s and remained married until his death 7 years ago. I believe society keeps on making divorce easier and easier. Maybe for me things could have worked out better if there had been rules and regulations before I could have filed for divorce. The government has made divorce an easy way out for people who just cannot deal with themselves anymore. Somewhere this process has to stop. Every day that I am alive, I tell my kids do not follow my example. I tell them to live their lives, go to college, get a job, be independent, and go and find their soul mate. Maybe this way they will not be a part of the statistics of divorce. I want my children to grow old with their mates. I want them to buy their first home together, and have children that grow with both parents. I never want to see my grandchildren suffer emotionally like I did or like I have caused my children to.

Something has to be done, to stop the epidemic of divorce. I believe that more should be done to prepare couples when they are getting ready to wed. I believe that couples should have to go through a regimen of classes, whether they are through the court or through the church—it really does not matter. This would eliminate issues that could potentially cause divorce.

Brandi – Religion 400 – The Christian Perspective – Capstone Course

Divorce is such an unpleasant word. When the word divorce is spoken, the first thought is always a negative one. In my opinion, divorce is not a good thing the majority of the time. I grew up in a home with divorced parents, and my dad lived in a different state, so I barely got to see him. It is rare in today's society to see someone who has parents that are not divorced. Honestly, divorce scares me—I don't want to end up like my parents and have a failed marriage. Divorce is so common in today's society that people don't even think twice about getting married, because if it does not work out, they can just get divorced, which I think is pointless and takes away the whole idea of marriage being sacred. Why even get married when you are just going to get divorced?

Alyssa – Religion 100 – Introduction to the Christian Faith

I have discovered in my short 20 years that the term "commitment" is not taken seriously. Growing up, my mother was my rock, she was strong and tough, but I watched the pain she endured from the divorce from both her second and third husbands (I was not alive when she divorced the first one). Although a wonderful woman, my mom has had commitment issues since I can remember.

From what I know, my parents stayed committed to each other during the relationships, as did my mother and stepfather, but eventually, the marriages both went south. I cannot say exactly what happened, because frankly I do not know. These days, I feel like relationships always fall apart. I have friends whose grandparents divorced after over 50 years. The lack of commitment in relationships has drastically changed the state of the family in the U.S.

Despite both divorces, my mom and I are still close, but now, the relationship with my dad has fallen apart. I remember being close to him before he moved out of our home; now his commitment to me has changed. It is a ripple effect; their commitment ended and in turn his commitment to his children ended. It may seem that I have an awfully bleak view of this topic, and well, I do.

…. Divorce not only affects the two people involved, but it affects the entire family. I can only go from my experiences, but after my mom and dad divorced, his family rarely spoke to us any more, and he stopped being a good parent to my brother and me. In my case though, this divorce did not stop my mom from caring for us. She has taught me how to be the person I am today. I think divorce affects family life a lot more when there are kids involved.

The divorce with my stepfather was not as bad because he was not our "real dad" (although he acts more like a father than my own); the pain was still there, but there was so much less fighting and stress. Divorce has such a negative effect on family life. Children have to deal with the stress of being shuffled between houses and being stereotyped as coming from a "broken home," while the adults often have to spend a lot of money from lawyer and court costs. Of course, there are divorces that are simple, but from what I have seen, they are most often not. I think that people often lean on divorce as an escape route without attempting to solve the problems. Granted, there are times when it is just easier to go your separate way, but I am sure that a lot of heartache and pain could be avoided if people would try to work out their issues.

Who Is God Here? Is Marriage a Human Construct? A Meditation on Isaiah 44:6-8

> Thus says the LORD, the King of Israel, and his Redeemer, the LORD of hosts: I am the first and I am the last; besides me there is no god. Who is like me? Let them proclaim it, let them declare and set it forth before me. Who has announced from of old the things to come? Let them tell us what is yet to be. Do not fear, or be afraid; have I not told you from of old and declared it? You are my witnesses! Is there any god besides me? There is no other rock; I know not one.

At stake in the present discussion is the nature of marriage—an order of creation ordained of God, or a human construct, emergent from culture and everywhere human-conditioned. God asserts His exclusive occupancy of the theological domain—"besides me there is no god."

About as blunt a statement as can be made: no other gods. The status and nature of marriage is first of all a theological question. "Babylonian pretenders," of whatever era, despite the success of their disciples, have not only no power, but also no existence. Such "gods" are fabrications of humanity, human constructs, artifacts made of precious ores and jewels, frozen in molded metal, chiseled in handsome stone. For his time, Isaiah continues (in succeeding verses) with his own observations: "All who make idols are nothing, and the things they delight in do not profit; their witnesses neither see nor know. And so they will be put to shame. Who would fashion a god or cast an image that can do no good? Look, all its devotees shall be put to shame; the artisans too are merely human. Let them all assemble, let them stand up; they shall be terrified, they shall all be put to shame."

To those who are God's witnesses, both ancient and current, we hear: "Do not fear, or be afraid; have I not told you from of old and declared it. You are my witnesses! Is there any god besides me? There is no other rock; I know not one." Only with impunity should we set out to construct other gods, but each of us does. In our time we have as many polytheists as atheists, following now and again one or another pretending deity in our ultimate concern granted to penultimate things. The most persistent pretender is our most intimate and cherished confidant: the person whom we see every morning in the mirror. Such a god had origin in Eden and manifestations globally. Such a god is ascendant in our time and in our country as premier arbiter of the Good, as to its content and as to warrant for doing it!

We are too sophisticated to fabricate a "god" that is declared so to be a god. Or are we? We come perilously close to the old self-conscious idolatry when we give theological legitimacy and liturgical voice to native spirits or religions, or allow tolerance to become *endorsement* in dialogue with other faiths, other gods. At stake, of course, is the status of other world religions, whether they are only idolatry, as the ancient Jews understood, along with Martin Luther and Karl Barth also, among others. Or whether they are different avenues to the only God who is God, as Tillich wanted to argue. Anything and everything from missions to morality is at stake in the matter. Do we have a story to tell to the nations, what has been told us of old? Or do we nestle in Babylon among the idols and give this one and that one credibility, or even allegiance? The oracle of God to the prophet is clear: Besides me there is no god. I am the first and the last. Let the one who has ears hear the word of the Lord.

In today's ecclesial climate of power and entertainment, with linguistic distortion of both the name of God and the content of the gospel, pabulum passing as content of the faith, privilege belonging to victims categorically, theocentric christology reducing Christ to one avenue among many (equally legitimate) avenues to God—in this climate it is tempting to invoke again the term

"Babylonian captivity of the church." Certainly those who are called to proclaim will have ample opportunity to give witness to Jesus Christ as their Lord and Savior, however they may or may not bite their tongues in order to stay within the strictures of the politically correct. But what of marriage? How can what God has declared— one man married to one woman—be one of two or more possible avenues of marital arrangement?

Christian faith affirms that marriage is an "order of creation," established by God in the manner of natural law, discernible "even to the gentiles, who do not have the Law." Instead, we note the attack upon the nature and meaning of marriage now by those who invoke the Light of the world to torture plain teaching of scripture. Marriage is today scorned by those who deem it "a patriarchal invention of power designed to subjugate women." And scorned even more by those who seek to make it other than one man, one woman. What is depicted in the Genesis account of creation as a God-ordained institution is reduced to a human construct, subject to deconstruction by those whose sensibilities are informed by primal urges variously described as "God's good gifts" and "according to my nature."

The erosion of marriage gained momentum during the latter half of the century just past. What passes now for toleration and liberation is in fact a challenge to the divine origins of marriage. Which raises the question: can God's blessing be invoked upon what God did not ordain? Indeed, can God's blessing be invoked upon relationships defined by acts that are παρα φυσίν ("against nature") (Romans 1:27ff), acts consistently repudiated by God through the teachings of His prophets and apostles? The now-familiar and increasingly sounded claim is that the Holy Spirit is "doing a new thing" in the movement to alter the nature of marriage. But the coherence resident in the Trinity does not allow conflicting teachings among the Three-in-One: the Son does not teach against the Father; the Holy Spirit does not teach against the Father and the Son. The Three are One and teach as One. The claim for the

19

Holy Spirit "doing a new thing" is not reform or repristination but innovation, for which there is no substantive precedent. Thus to invoke the blessing of God upon relationships other than one man and one woman is a violation of marriage as God so ordained.

The Fourth Evangelist begins the ministry of the Incarnate Lord in Cana, at a wedding. He was there, celebrating marriage. It was not at a bar mitzvah, or a wake, or a feast of tabernacles—but at a wedding. Its setting is material and human, couched in celebration, as well as in practical matters like "enough wine" and "good wine." Jesus' presence at the Cana marriage feast gives incarnational endorsement to marriage as ordained of God, an Order of Creation.

Marriage and Divorce

Meditation on Genesis 2:18-24 and Mark 10:2-12

Genesis 2:18-24 – Then the LORD God said, "it is not good that the man should be alone; I will make him a helper fit for him." Out of the ground the LORD God formed every beast of the field and every bird of the air, and brought them to the man to see what he would call them and whatever the man called every living creature, that was its name. The man gave names to all cattle, and to the birds of the air and to every beast of the field; but for the man there was not found a helper fit for him. So the LORD God caused a deep sleep to fall upon the man, and while he slept took one of his ribs and closed up its place with flesh; and the rib which the LORD God had taken from the man he made into a woman and brought her to the man. Then the man said, "This at last is bone of my bones and flesh of my flesh; she shall be called Woman, because she was taken out of Man. Therefore a man leaves his father and his mother and cleaves to his wife and they become one flesh."

Mark 10:2-12 – And Pharisees came up and in order to test him asked, "Is it lawful for a man to divorce his wife?" He answered them, "What did Moses command you"? They said, "Moses allowed a man to write a certificate of divorce, and to put her away." But Jesus said to them, "For your hardness of heart he wrote you this commandment. But from the beginning of creation, 'God made them male and female.' 'For this reason a man shall leave his father and mother and be joined to his wife, and the two shall become one.' So they are no longer two but one. What therefore God has joined together, let not man put asunder." And in the house the disciples asked him again about this matter. And he said to them, "Whoever divorces his wife and marries another, commits adultery against her; and if she divorces her husband and marries another she commits adultery."

These passages have as a common theme the nature of marriage. In Genesis 2, God creates woman as a helper fit for the man, an origin cited by Jesus to the Pharisees who try in the Gospel to test him on the teaching about divorce. The old liturgy of the *Service Book and Hymnal* (SBH) properly announced marriage as a "holy estate, ordained of God…, to be held in honor by all" (270). The *Lutheran Book of Worship* (LBW) recalls that "the Lord God in his goodness created us male and female, and by the gift of marriage founded human community in a joy that begins now and is brought to perfection in the life to come" (203). Tertullian (in *Exhortations on Chastity*) argued that not only *marriage* but *monogamy* is established in the creation. One man and one woman, in the image of God created He them.

The content of Genesis 2 is especially important in our time, on three accounts, the second and the third presupposed by the first. First, at stake is the nature of marriage as to its origin and status. Second, the question of divorce and its fracture of marriage. Third, the question of what *constitutes* marriage—one man and one woman, or some other combination of two or more.

The Bible couches the estate of marriage as a gift of God to humanity, from the beginning. God instituted marriage as one man

21

and one woman—Hebrew patriarchs and kings, along with Joseph Smith and the other early latter-day saints, notwithstanding. The first command of the scriptures ("be fruitful and multiply, and fill the earth and subdue it") presupposes marriage, it being unthinkable that God should command to multiply those whom He has also not also previously blessed by marriage. Cultural anthropologists concede that some form of marriage is indigenous to human culture, in virtually every instance of investigation, but would argue that the arrangement is, like language, culturally emergent, as necessary to human community and survival as gathering or producing food.

The nature of marriage thus emerges as first a theological question: is marriage, like the sky and sea and grass and the law of gravity, first of all a creation of God, more or less well (or badly) appropriated and lived by peoples of every time and every place? Or is it, like capitalism or socialism, a system of organization invented by humanity to make things work a little better (or worse), as a "safe place" for children to be born into and grow up?

Christians affirm that marriage is God's creation, God's gift, His promise—rather than simply some convenient and rational way of ordering things like sexual access, responsibility for children, and making a living. And, not least, a foundation for regulating property (both real and personal). If God created marriage and ordained it for humankind, then it carries a different status than if it is only a human construct, such as a particular economic system. Just as the *imago dei* mandates a different way of dealing with human beings than a view that sees us as "wingless, relatively hairless bipeds" (Desmond Morris, *The Naked Ape*). One may write an *ethic* of economic fairness, or an *ethic* for assessing political systems. But one must start with a *theology* of marriage, because of its origins in the mandates of God.

The second dimension is divorce and its fracture of marriage. This is the question posed to Jesus by the Pharisees, they knowing full well both the Genesis ordination and the Moses concession.

Jesus "up'd the ante" with his theological assertion: "What therefore God has joined together, let not man put asunder." Moses, he said, made the concession (to the aspect of divorce) because of the hardness of their hearts. When His disciples asked Him again about the matter, in the house, He put the teaching even stronger: "Whoever divorces his wife and marries another, commits adultery against her; and if she divorces her husband and marries another, she commits adultery." The New Testament and the early church are no less stringent. To divorce is to sin.

Is marriage harmed by divorce? Of course. Both in general and in particular. What is wanting is more and better counsel and commitment on the front end: preparation, nurture, counseling, persons who continue to monitor and measure their relationship—and who take pains to be faithful, not just in matters sexual, but in "all matters before the house." And repentance, both on account of the divorce and in serious reflection, in the case that one should consider remarriage.

The third factor is perhaps the most controversial in our time: what *constitutes* marriage? A man and a woman? Surely. There is, of course, an insurgency that wants both the church and the state to regard and recognize, in the manner of marriage, gay unions and lesbian unions. In the Lutheran tradition this issue has provoked schism—schism, I would argue—by the ones who have abandoned the teaching of the one, holy, catholic and apostolic church.

One argument from the revisionists is to note that the nature of marriage has been changed (or at least eroded) by the possibility of its being undertaken a second time, or even a third or fourth, with the church's recognition. Therefore, the argument goes, if the nature of marriage has been changed as to the possibility of *remarriage after divorce*, then the nature of marriage as to its *constituents* is open to change as well.

23

There is an important and exclusionary distinction, however: as noted above, no one doubts that divorce is caused by sin and is itself a reflection of sin. Divorce is a sin. But marriage itself is not sin. Unlike marriage, what is being proposed—and here and there adopted, as by the ELCA—concerning expanding the constituency to two men or two women, has no biblical endorsement. Homogenital behavior, of whatever sort, whether committed or casual or predatory or that remarked by St. Paul in Romans 1 of men "being *consumed with passion* for one another," is forbidden and is called what it is: sin. Marriage itself, though burdened by sin, is of the creation (Genesis 1 & 2), rather than of the fall of man. Marriage consists of a man and a woman. Not two of the same sex. And certainly not three or more in either or both sexes—any of which is in principle possible if marriage is not one man, one woman as God ordained.

Ours is a time made difficult by confusion, not least by a conception of freedom that insists on personal and individual definitions of truth. The theological truth of marriage is that it is an order of creation, ordained by God, to be held in honor by all. We may not alter what is marriage, because it is God-ordained. Again, it is an order of creation, the first (initial) of the orders of creation, directly involving human beings. We may, with fear and trembling, recognize that repentance and amendment of life are possible, and "the joy of marriage can be restored" for those whose marriages are troubled, even for those whose lives have been broken. That is no concession; it resides, rather, in forgiveness...following repentance, amendment of life, and courage. And, I think, grace.

The Christian Scriptures begin and end with marriage—in creation and in the eschaton, in the marriage feast of the Lamb (Revelation 19). Isaiah's depiction of the restoration of Zion resides in the same relationship of intimacy and celebration. Zion is no more desolate or forsaken but *married* and a source of delight to the LORD (Isaiah 54). In the coming eschatological future, which Isaiah invokes even within the desolation of history, those who have by

God's grace become those in whom the Lord delights, hear the words: "with everlasting love I will have compassion on you" (Isaiah 54:8). Thanks be to God!

The Abortion Abomination

One suspects that to the "ears of God" the silent pills and suction devices of abortions are as loud and as hellish as nail-shrapnel bombs. But to the popular press and media, whose inclination is to embrace and glorify a distorted understanding of personal freedom, the bombs are the attraction. The victims are much more easy to find, and easy to claim.

Jeremiah 1:5 "Before I formed you in the womb I knew you, and before you were born I consecrated you." Is it only Jeremiah that the Lord knows before He is formed in the womb? Either as to prophetic calling, or as to now-and-again wailing reluctance or, foundationally, as to being? Is it only thus Jeremiah that the Lord knows before He forms him in the womb?

I think not. St. Paul says, and cogently: "...so, there is no distinction. All have sinned and fall short of the glory of God" (Romans 3:23). So also, from the point of view of a "child of God," as to creation and as to ontology, there is no distinction: both theologically and naturally speaking, all human beings are children of God, "known" in the womb before they are born.

Developmentally and ontologically speaking, all genetic material is, in principle, in place, from the moment of conception. There is thus no debate, theologically and ontologically: aborting a "fetus," aborting a child, is taking a life. One cannot make a case, on theological grounds, for the procedure, for the phenomenon.

The cultural and now legal conceit that an abortion is reducible to a "choice" to "terminate a pregnancy" ignores the plain truth resident in the equation. In most all other dimensions of life, the notions of process and developmentalism prevail. In abortion, ontology and development are bracketed—ignored—in the interest of the "choice." Sexual license has been the more liberated by various means to prevent pregnancy...and factors of both passion and carelessness yield the more unwanted pregnancies. Ergo, another candidate for abortion. "Before I formed you in the womb I knew you."

Kyrie eleison. Christe eleison. Kyrie eleison.

Catechesis as Amendment of Life

A reasonable translation of Martin Luther's response after having toured the parishes in the locale of Wittenberg is "Good God, what wretchedness I beheld." The wretchedness of both ignorance and sin led him to pen the *Small Catechism*, to be taught by the parents—actually, the head of the family—to both the children and the adults of the home.

Luther made his tour at the end of the seventh decade in a world that knew the printing press. Illiteracy yet compounded willful ignorance. Reductionist legalism compounded a facile faith with oppressive guilt. Luther wrote the *Small Catechism* to be a primer of the faith, a primer that both conveyed and examined the fundamentals: The Ten Commandments and their meanings, the Apostles' Creed as to both articles and explanations. The Lord's Prayer, by petitions and articulation of meaning. The Sacrament of Baptism by definition, by institution, and by articulation of meaning. The Sacrament of Holy Communion—the Holy Eucharist, by institution, and by articulation, and by exploration of meaning. The Office of the Keys and Confession – again by definitions and articulation of meaning.

The introduction of the *Small Catechism* proved an indispensable dimension of the forward movement of the Reformation. The

Catechism put explanatory contemporary content to the commandments, the sacraments, the creed, and the Lord's Prayer. Taught in the home, the content served to inform both worship and piety. The *Small Catechism* intruded into a pervasive ignorance born of both poverty and blight.

The need today for rejuvenation, even in some places, *re-introduction* of the Catechism has not to do with a poverty of either means or stimuli. The information age, the age of instant communication, internet, Twitter, Facebook, all these combine to make scarce any attention to learning any things ethical, much less creedal.

In today's religious climate, which is a mind-boggling miasma of twists and innovations and retrogressions, people going off in all directions to mix and match in their own fancies, it is incumbent on Christian pastors to proclaim the orthodox faith, as St. Paul instructs: "Now, brothers, I want to remind you of the gospel I preached to you, which you received and on which you have taken your stand. By this gospel you are saved, if you hold firmly to the word I preached to you. Otherwise, you have believed in vain. For what I received I passed on to you as of first importance: that Christ died for our sins according to the Scriptures, that he was buried, that he was raised on the third day according to the Scriptures..." (I Cor. 15:1-4). Christ is Risen! He is risen indeed, Alleluia!

The articulation of marriage as an order of creation, as an estate ordained of God needs not only to be taught and proclaimed, but also lived. Marriage is not reducible to a cultural construct, a patriarchal invention of power designed to subjugate women, or a matriarchal invention of security designed to corral the male libido by exchanging access for exclusivity. Marriage is "ordained by God, to be held in honor by all, and it becomes those who enter therein to weigh with reverent minds what the Word of God teaches concerning it."

Essential Rubrics – a few from 45 years...

Postscript – Foundational

- God ordained and blessed marriage, and, although many a cross has been laid thereon, continues still thus to bless.

- The thread that Marianne and Larry seek to find and follow: Foundational to marriage is striving to keep God's moral law—foundational to marriage, 'til death do us part.

- The most loving thing a father and mother can do for their children is to love the Lord.

- The next most loving thing a father can do for his children is to love their mother.

- Marriage is God + one man + one woman.

- Family is God + one man + one woman + children + grandchildren, *deo volente.*

- The glue, the thread, the "tie that binds" is God and His commandments.

Postscript – Implementing

- We know that the head of the household is, first of all, the Lord. Both husband and wife understand this, rather than one or the other seizing power, or attempting to.

- One keeps his vows. One keeps her vows.

- One respects the other as equal in principle, and equal in fact.

- One tells the truth.

- One absolutely does not violate fidelity as to a third party.

- The couple plans together—there are times when the agenda shifts prominently to one or the other, for graduate school, for employment, for child rearing, for any number of other questions of priority—and respect is as much or more the content of love as is ardor.

- One respects the other's likes and dislikes. Learn to handle disagreements amicably.

- Learn to quarrel without rancor, or radically impugning the integrity or the humanity of the other.

- Decide the dimensions and boundaries for handling both sets of in-laws.

- Decide who handles what. Never impugn each other.

- Discover and employ ways of having fun together—physically, mentally, and emotionally.

- Take turns with handling the finances, house-cleaning, daily chores etc. to such an extent that each one knows how to handle them in case of emergency.

- The two learn together. The two grow together.

- In all the dimensions of life that "count" there is foundational and thoroughgoing equality.

- There is trust in truth telling, trust in finances, trust in mutual respect.

- Understand that you are the other's best friend. And build that friendship on the solid rock of Christ.

Appendix A: LR Student Response:

Stephen – Religion 340 – Modern Theology

In the past fifty years, American views of sexuality, marriage and the value of life have undergone a dramatic shift. The cultural revolution of the 1960s and early 1970s was a response to the cold, repressed, shallow post-war American consumerism which left many feeling as though traditional values were meaningless and traditional views of marriage served only to stifle one's natural sex drive and oppress women by keeping them at home and under the authority and domination of men. Many of the youth of the era reacted in quite a radical way to the admittedly stifling atmosphere. In the process however, they did irreparable damage to the institution of marriage and in their gratuitous shirking of tradition purely for the sake of progress rather than reason.

What the youth of the Cultural Revolution were seeking, were freedom, enlightenment, and meaning (all of which were certainly lacking in the post-war Eisenhower-era conservatism of the 1950s). Unfortunately, what was accomplished through the undermining of tradition was a social catastrophe which left a generation of children from divided homes unable to form meaningful relationships. Women of the era found new freedom from old oppression, but in the process the dignity of femininity was aborted through the devaluation of motherhood. The yield of the Cultural Revolution was essentially the same as the yield of post-war conservatism—the creation and perpetuation of a culture of death.

As a Christian in today's post-Cultural Revolution, post-Liberal, post-post-modern world; one finds oneself in search, not of what was lost as a result of the Cultural Revolution, but of what never was—a culture of life. This culture of life is not found in oppressive conservatism-for-the-hell-of-it, nor is it found in a philosophy which would perpetuate a holocaust against the unborn under the guise of a "woman's right to choose." Indeed, there is error in both camps with regard to something essential—the humanity of the individual. In the first place, there is no dignity in a marriage in which one spouse is subservient to the other, nor is there dignity in the notion that marriage is but an arrangement of convenience free from commitment. If indeed a culture is to be created in which all humanity is viewed as having intrinsic dignity, it must begin with a view of marriage as committed and essential to the structure of family and society. Since family is essential for the procreation and education of children, logic would dictate that if a culture of life is to be created, it will be done first in the homes.

One of the most hotly debated issues to be addressed is the question of abortion and what it means to be truly "pro-life." Any idiot with a thinking mind and knowledge of potentiality and actuality is anti-abortion. Frankly, it may well be that the hypocrisy of a movement which calls itself "pro-life" while simultaneously pursuing social and economic policies which perpetuate poverty, the death penalty and unjust wars does equal damage to the dignity and sacredness of life as those who have declared "open season" on those in the womb. Thus the notion of "pro-life" being used simply in regard to ending the holocaust against the unborn is rather misleading.

If there is to truly be a universal affirmation of the intrinsic dignity and value of humanity, then one must not only affirm that the unborn have the right to life, but the right to a life which is livable. This includes the right to a living wage, the right to universal medical treatment, the right to worship one's conscience, the right to a livable environment, freedom of speech, and freedom to pursue one's dreams.

Included in this affirmation of dignity is also the intrinsic right of persons with homosexual orientation, or bisexual orientation to live honestly and without fear of persecution. In the pre-Cultural Revolution culture of the US, those with homosexual orientation needed not be told that they were going to hell; frankly, they were already there. Hate crimes were commonplace and the American Psychological Association considered the orientation to be a psychological illness. The churches did not help matters and often made things worse by railing against the sin of sodomy with a violence which did far more damage to the dignity of human life than the act itself ever could. The result of this was a gay community which became gradually more anti-religious and anti-traditional, not because they themselves devalued human life, but because the value of their humanity had been devalued by the establishments of the day. Certainly, the Church must always hold to the teachings of Scripture and to Tradition, and surely the act of sodomy IS a sin (thus marriage can never be defined as between two persons of the same gender since a sacrament cannot be party to a mortal sin). The issue is not the teaching of the Scriptures, NOR is it in the natural orientation of the individual (homosexuality after all does occur in nature and therefore cannot be said to be simply a matter of choice); the issue is that the dignity of the person must always be respected, regardless of sin and that all persons must be welcomed with kindness and sensitivity both to personhood and to Scripture.

Ultimately, that the nuclear family has had a meltdown is not the result of the Cultural Revolution, it is a result of the failure of that revolution. What was attempted was the formation of a society of freedom, dignity, and love; what ensued were chaos, greater damage to human dignity both on the part of progressives (who pursued sexual immorality and abortion) and conservatives (who sought to perpetuate the capitalist mentality which was equally degrading to humanity.). Both failed, both are in error, and both are guilty of creating the mess which is the current state of marriage and of life in general in the US. What is required is a second cultural revolution; not one to undo the first but one which will accomplish what previous cultures failed to do—to live, to thrive and to love as God loves.

Appendix B: An Overt Challenge

From: David (.........)
Sent: Monday, August 09, 2010 11:33 PM (e-mail)
To: Larry Yoder
Cc: Lenoir-Rhyne University President's Cabinet
Subject: ELCA

Dr. Yoder:

I recently attended a presentation you gave on leaving the ELCA and joining Lutheran CORE. As an alumni [sic] of LR [an ELCA school], I was embarrassed by your obvious dislike of the

ELCA and your desire for our congregation to leave the ELCA. I am also disturbed by the fact that you are both advocating congregations leave the ELCA while teaching at an ELCA institution.

I certainly respect academic debate, but I am concerned about your obvious political objectives. I also wonder why you advocate leaving the same institution that pays your salary. The bishop also did a presentation which was quite factual and non-biased; however, your presentation was amazingly biased and makes me wonder about your motives.

If I were an "average" member of a congregation whose only interaction with LR was your presentation, I would think twice about donating to LR, approving congregational support of LR, and suggesting that young people attend the school. I certainly hope that your views are not reflective of the view of Lenoir-Rhyne. I was disappointed by your presentation and am certainly embarrassed for the reputation of Lenoir-Rhyne.

I hope in the future you consider the school and its reputation.

Sincerely,

David (...name withheld...)

August 10, 2010 – also e-mail

Mr. (...),

First a few clarifications as to your letter:

• I went to (church, town), to the meeting that you attended, at the invitation of the Congregation Council, which was conveyed in a phone call from Pastor (.....)

• Each congregation (or each individual) must decide, according to the "bound conscience" concept as referenced in the ELCA documents.

• I made no advocacy, no case for leaving the ELCA... I was asked to talk about Lutheran CORE and North American Lutheran Church and did precisely that. I did not suggest that (congregation) either join Lutheran CORE or leave the ELCA. In fact, congregations (and individuals) can join Lutheran CORE *without* leaving the ELCA. Lutheran CORE is a "free-standing synod," not a church body.

• I explained various dimensions attendant to the issues of provocation, and the factors attendant to joining Lutheran CORE and/or the North American Lutheran Church.

• In short, I made no overt advocacy to join anything.

In response to your points and in some expansion of what I said at (church):

My quarrel with the ELCA—not so much "dislike" (as you frame it) but radical disagreement and disappointment—is theological and ecclesial, not "political," as you suggest.

The ELCA action in Minneapolis in 2009 constitutes at the foundational level a theological and biblical issue of the first order: it challenges and alters the content of what constitutes marriage, as articulated by Jesus, when he addressed God's intent as to the nature of marriage in the context of an inquiry put to him about divorce:

> Have you not read that he who made them at the beginning made them male and female, and said, 'For this cause a man shall leave his father and mother and cleave to his wife, and the twain shall become one flesh. Wherefore they are no more twain but one flesh? What therefore God has joined together, let not man put asunder (Matthew 19:4-6).

What the ELCA thus "sundered" in the Minneapolis vote was the *nature of marriage* as constituted by husband and wife, man and woman. In other words, by including relationships other than "male and female" to count, in effect, as marriage for ELCA pastors, the

ELCA has foundationally altered, by expansion, what the Bible teaches as the constitutive nature of marriage.

That is a theological move that profoundly affects cardinal dimensions of the faith: it alters the content of the sixth commandment; challenges the authority of God to make commandments in the first place; alters the first article of the Apostles Creed as to what is thus "blessed" in God's good creation; alters the second article of the Creed as to what does and does not require repentance, *per se*, for the relationship; and alters the third article by expanding "what counts as marriage" in the one, holy, catholic, and apostolic church.

In understanding those theological dimensions that way, I am in the company of leading ELCA theologians and ethicists, among them most prominently Carl Braaten, James Nestingen, and Robert Benne...all of whom have written in a similar vein concerning the theological dimensions.

As to the ecclesial dimensions, the Minneapolis action affects the whole of the ELCA, insofar as to "where we stand" concerning that kind of relationship. What the American culture is coming more frequently to tolerate—even embrace—the ELCA has now also included in its clergy policy by this action.

In our doctrine of the church (i.e., our ecclesiology) we have understood ourselves as a "body of Christ in the Church Catholic," rather than an aggregate of parishes. The Minneapolis action, in effect, makes the ELCA an "aggregate" in this one area, where congregations can individually vote to accept or refuse clergy of the sort of relationship named.

But, in principle, the ELCA has approved such relationships and considers them thus in the manner of marriage. A congregation does not alter the *principle* by refusing to accept the *option*. All ELCA congregations are, in principle, members of a church that accepts and blesses such relationships.

Behind and informing the ELCA action is a reading of scripture that ignores the biblical teaching against such behavior. The ELCA action is predicated under "new understanding" not resident—or legitimately possible—from the text, or the biblical context.

And, in the Scriptures, it is the *behavior* that is restricted, not the person. Persons of homosexual *orientation* are welcome in congregations that are voting to join the North American Lutheran Church – on the same grounds as all heterosexual persons ... that is, as repentant sinners seeking God's grace and mercy at the foot of the cross. What is rejected in Lutheran CORE and the North American Lutheran Church is *not persons but behaviors.*

My "objectives" are thus foundational and thoroughly theological, ethical and ecclesial. The only "political" dimension arises when one asks, "what am I to do?" – given the circumstances.

I and others can neither embrace nor ignore what we consider to be plainly against the teaching of the Holy Scriptures and the One, Holy, Catholic and Apostolic Church across the ages. Our consciences are thus bound to the Word of God, a concept deeply embedded in Lutheran theology. Several of my clergy colleagues— and a few laity—have "swum the Tiber" to Rome (i.e., have joined the Roman Catholic Church), most recently Dr. Michael Root of Lutheran Southern Seminary. Others have gone—or are considering going—to the Lutheran Church–Missouri Synod.

The movement toward forming the North American Lutheran Church has developed from conversations, particularly in Lutheran CORE and WordAlone, and among persons not affiliated with either group but nonetheless seeking theological and ecclesial coherence.

As I said earlier, my remarks at (church) were made at the request of the Church Council. My comments at that level were reportorial and explanatory. When asked, I spoke plainly what I intend, as to path. I did not attempt to speak on behalf of anyone else. I did not attempt to speak in behalf of Lenoir-Rhyne.

As to representing Lenoir-Rhyne, to my knowledge the institution has taken no formal position on the matter, following thus the ELCA principle of "local acceptance or rejection, or received without comment," regarding what was voted in Minneapolis. (Note: soon after receiving the copies of this exchange, the university president announced to the faculty, at the conclusion to his opening remarks of the semester, that the university would abide by the vote of the Minneapolis ELCA decision.) I have little doubt that the action of the ELCA will have some effect on institutions of the church, if for no other reason than a decline in congregational offerings.

But Lenoir-Rhyne, as an institution of higher learning, embraces the principle of academic freedom. As a faculty member and a theologian/ethicist, I am obliged to study the issues and to articulate the various dimensions. My speaking at (church) was precisely what the Pastor asked me to do: articulate the position of those who oppose the Minneapolis action. And the Bishop was invited to offer the case for the Synod, measuring "both sides," with an obvious case for "accommodation."

(With regard to "schism," some debate legitimately exists as to who precisely are the schismatics: the ones who favor the vote that fractures the received understanding of marriage, or the ones whose disagreement with that vote obliges them to seek other ecclesial venues! From the point of view of the teachings of the One, Holy, Catholic, and Apostolic Church, it is the action of the ELCA Minneapolis assembly that departs the Tradition.)

One does not "embarrass" his institution by an articulate presentation of the issues, from the point of view from which he is asked to speak. And one does not abandon his convictions—and the content of his faith—when the foundations of the faith are on the line. As to advocacy, I did not attempt to tell the persons present what they should do.

In regard to "considering the school and its reputation" – as a great-great nephew of one of the founders, I always consider the school. Marianne and I are both graduates, as are our three sons, two of our three daughters-in-law (one of them yet only engaged, but with date set), as are my brother and one of his two sons, my sister and brother-in-law and their two sons, my sainted mother, several of my aunts and uncles and numerous Yoder cousins in the Catawba Valley and environs.

But in the hierarchy of loyalties, wife and family come before institution…and conscience—bound to the content of the faith in Father, Son, and Holy Spirit—comes highest of all.

Equally sincerely,

J. Larry Yoder

Appendix C: "Moving on from the Wilderness of Sin" … Exodus 17:1

"Israel moved on from the wilderness of Sin by stages." Would that it were so! That we, like Israel, could move on from the wilderness of Sin by *stages*. Like Laurence Kohlberg and the stages of moral development: analytical, developmental, manageable (or at least coachable), achievable… even perhaps perfectible. More the better if the wilderness of Sin were for us some geography of the land instead of the soul, some terrain to be traversed instead of rebellious metastasis in the mind.

But the metaphor of hardness of heart … is an apt one for the wilderness of sin. How could the Israelites, witnesses to the ten plagues, delivered by the Passover, hikers across dry sea, recipients of manna and quail—how could these folk doubt Moses' leadership and "put God to the proof"? They were, after all, participants in a spiritual migration of covenant proportions. Human nature is ever the same. Obedience is overcome by contempt at the tree in the garden, contempt at the rock in the wilderness: Give us fruit, give us power, give us water! Whatever.…..

"Why do you put the Lord to the test?" Why indeed!! Because of this hardness of heart. This is not mere petulance. It is revolt, this time a revolt born of thirst, born of the reality of wandering in a harsh climate, born in a pilgrimage easier to understand in the comfort of memory than when in the midst of it. The revolt is more a challenge to God than to Moses. The *moreso* to God, in that Moses has at every turn credited God for the exodus: "the God of Abraham, Isaac, and Jacob, Who brought you *up* out of the land of Egypt."

The Rev. J. Larry Yoder, PhD, STS, is Professor of Theology and Director, Center for Theology, at Lenoir-Rhyne University; Interim Pastor (1992-present), Grace Lutheran Church, Newton, NC; and Dean, Carolinas Chapter, Society of the Holy Trinity. He is a pastor in the North American Lutheran Church, Carolinas Chapter.

Understanding the Hostile Environment to Marriage in God's Plan

F. B. Henry, Bishop of Calgary

What is meant by the hostile environment to marriage in God's plan? I want to cite several factors that have contributed to that environment.

- In the wake of the sexual revolution the divine institution of marriage has been deconstructed by easy and quick divorce laws.

- It has been trivialized by the prevalence of cohabitation or "living together" as a substitute for matrimony.

- It has been poisoned by the widespread practice of contraception.

- It has been attacked as an obsolete, oppressive patriarchal institution which has enslaved women and reduced their roles to menial work.

- It has been perverted and neutered by the advocates of same-sex marriages who reject the traditional meaning of matrimony as the union of a man and a woman.

- And it has been marginalized by the careerists and professionals who delay and postpone marriage and children for a higher standard of living and a more affluent lifestyle.

I would ask you to not only take note of the sexual revolution, cohabitation, contraception, a patriarchal institution, same-sex marriages, and careerism, but especially the powerful verbs: deconstructed, trivialized, poisoned, attacked, perverted and neutered, and marginalized.

In 1947, Reverend John Hugo, a theologian and retreat leader with Dorothy Day's Catholic Worker Movement, described "the spiritual condition of our people" in these strikingly familiar terms:

> It is customary for some to take a rosy view [of American Catholic life] ... basing their optimism on tables of statistics concerning the growth of the Catholic population, the income and resources of the Church, the number of communions, etc. But such a method of computation is very unreliable where spiritual realities are concerned. Were it of any value, we could compute the degree of religious fervor from the quantities of grease burnt in votive stands, and our optimism would soar to the very skies.... [But] even in the case of those who are wholly faithful to the external obligations of religion, there is often little evidence, aside from their devotions, that they are living Christian lives. Large areas of their lives are wholly unilluminated by their faith. Their ideas, their attitudes, their views on current affairs, their pleasure and recreations, their tastes in reading and entertainment, their love of luxury, comfort and bodily ease, their devotion to success, their desire of money, their social snobbishness, racial consciousness, nationalistic narrowness and prejudice, their bourgeois complacency and contempt of the poor: In all these things they are indistinguishable from the huge sickly mass of paganism which surrounds them (*Weapons of the Spirit: Selected Writings of Father John Hugo*).

Written sixty years ago, Hugo's words ring even truer today. I am going to make the substitution of "Christian" for "Catholics" as we have all made ourselves indistinguishable from our non-Christian neighbours. We have the same virtues and vices. And this is why the culture isn't more "Christian," even though we make up the majority of the population. A kind of foggy worldliness has settled into the Christian soul. In effect, a great many Christians keep the Christian brand name, but they freelance what it means.

The point is this: Christians now face a crisis of faith, mission, and leadership—and the task of fixing it falls *equally* on all disciples, laity and clergy alike.

Too many Christians seem to assume a guaranteed grounding of success, stability, energy, and security for the church that is arguably eroding right out from under them. In fact, we face very serious questions about our future; questions that lack any easy programmatic answers.

Every new beginning must start with a return to Jesus Christ, the Gospel, and the Church. The heart of renewal is pretty straightforward: Do we *really* believe that Jesus Christ is our savior? Do we *really* believe that the Gospels are the Word of God? Do we *really* believe that the Church was by founded Christ himself, and that she teaches in his name? Many of us who call ourselves "Christian" live as if we'd never really thought about any of these questions. In fact, by our actions, many of us witness a kind of practical atheism: paying lip service to God, but living as if He didn't exist. Many of us don't really believe we need a savior. In fact, we don't see anything we need to be *saved from.*

Renewal begins from the inside out. That applies equally to persons and societies. Every one of us, every day, must start again to "repent and believe in the Gospel." That means accepting the truth that we need Jesus Christ in our lives—that he is our only salvation; that his Gospel is the only way to live; and that his church

43

is our mother and guide. These interior acts of faith are not empty pieties. When sincere, they will always have external, public consequences. As the epistle says, *"We have seen and testify that the Father has sent his Son as the Savior of the world"* (1 John 4:14).

Renewal means that we must take a hard look at *how* we proclaim and live our Christian faith in this culture.

Too many Christians have unconsciously come to see the church through the lens of secular politics; to falsely divide the "institutional" church from an imaginary "real" church. Too many Christians use the church as an arena in which interest-group battles are fought out while organizing lobbies and pressure blocs, demonizing ideological opponents, and interpreting relationships largely in terms of power. None of this has anything to do with authentic ecclesiology, and it's a temptation that infects nearly all parties in the church, no matter what their point of departure—left or right. This may be the most distressing example of how assimilation to our secular culture has produced distortions in Christian life, of which we're only dimly aware and that now require a huge effort of reevangelization.

All of us, laity and clergy alike, need to admit that we've been too naive, too often. The Protestant theologian Stanley Hauerwas once warned that the great weakness of Christian witness in our time is that we preach as though we don't have enemies. But we do.

In our legitimate hopes for a role in the life of our society, Christians have ignored an unpleasant truth: that there are active, motivated groups in modern society that bitterly resent the Christian Gospel, and would like to silence it and its adherents.

In the words of the Vietnamese archbishop (later cardinal) F. X. Nguyen Van Thuan: *"The greatest failure in leadership is for the leader to be afraid to speak and act as a leader."* Van Thuan had been a bishop only a year when Saigon fell to the communists in 1975. The new regime locked him in forced-labor camps and prisons for thirteen years. He spent the last nine in solitary confinement, in a vermin-infested cell with no windows. Yet he was a leader even in his captivity. Under pain of death, he celebrated the Eucharist with bread and wine smuggled in to him. He wrote words of encouragement and hope that he smuggled out to his people.

We face none of the direct persecution that so many Christians around the world routinely endure. We might be more alive if we did. Instead, we're weighed down by distraction, indifference, and comfort; by all the moral narcotics that come with an open and materially abundant society. It's an old problem but with a new twist.

First of all, it is an old problem It comes whenever the Church and her people begin to get too comfortable as part of society's structures. Saint Hilary, bishop of Poitiers, wrote about it in the fourth century (*Against the Emperor Constantius*):

> But today we fight an insidious persecutor, an enemy who flatters.... He does not stab us in the back but fills our stomachs. He does not seize our property and thereby give us life. He stuffs our pockets to lead us to death. He does not cast us into dungeons thereby setting us on the path to freedom. He imprisons us in the honors of the palace. He showers priests with honors, so that there will be no good bishops. He builds churches that he may destroy the faith.

Most of us have food to eat and work that puts cash in our pockets. We have money to build churches, access to lawmakers, and talented, influential people in our communities. Our achievements and hard work give us a unique power to bear witness to the Gospel. But we often face enormous counter pressures to stay silent, to compromise on matters of justice, to go along with fashionable opinion.

45

We can take a lesson from the early church. The emperor Valens ruled the eastern half of the Roman Empire in the 360s AD. He was a brutal man at a time of bitter political and religious turmoil, and he sought to destroy the orthodox faith in Christ. Saint Basil the Great, then the bishop of Caesarea, confronted him face-to-face about his policies. "Never has anyone dared to speak to me with such freedom," Valens said. Basil replied, "Obviously you have never met a bishop before" (Rahner, *Church and State in Early Christianity*).

This is how Christians must lead: with candor, simplicity, and courage. In every situation, men and women must know that they have "met a bishop." Not a privileged dignitary, not a corporate executive; but a leader and teacher, a true apostle of Jesus Christ. Something similar is true for every lay Christian. People should come away from every encounter with us knowing that they have met a true *Christian*.

Too often in recent decades, Christians, both clergy and lay, have made ourselves guilty of "kneeling before the world," in Jacques Maritain's famous words. We find ourselves softening the Christian message—the cross, the call to holiness, the reality that all men and women are under the judgment of God—because these truths aren't considered respectful in a secularized, pluralistic society.

One pervasive form of this genuflection to the world is a pragmatic "reductionism" in offering the Gospel. To gain a public hearing, many Christians find themselves explaining and justifying the church's social teachings in practical, *humanitarian* terms.

Pope John Paul II knew this kind of false compromise very well:

> The temptation today is to reduce Christianity to merely
> human wisdom, a pseudo-science of well-being. In our
> heavily secularized world a "gradual secularization of

salvation" has taken place, so that people strive for the good of man, but man who is truncated, reduced to his merely horizontal dimension (*Redemptio Missio*, 11).

Secondly, it's an old problem with a new twist.

The new twist is the aggressive attempt, not merely to silence or marginalize religious belief and its influence, but to demolish it altogether and enshrine a completely new moral order based on Pluralism, Secularism and Individualism.

Pluralism

Harvard's Pluralism Project defines pluralism as "the engagement that creates a common society" from the colourful diversity we see all around us. Pluralism teaches us to celebrate our differences, and indeed becomes an instrument for ensuring, as Avigail Eisenberg puts it, "that no one principle, ideal, or way of life can dominate."

In this way of thinking there are no moral norms or absolutes, no natural order or laws that bind human beings to their humanity. Pluralism itself is the only imperative, the only absolute – the one principle that will, after all, dominate.

Pluralism, in other words, is not so much a practical response to changing demographics and increased immigration, as it is a tactic in the culture war. It is a technique for disenfranchising the majority who still respect natural law, although it pretends to be celebrating or enhancing social diversity.

Of course, Christianity is not against diversity. Indeed, its Trinitarian theology and its doctrine of creation arguably provide the only real foundation for respect for the many and not merely for the one, for the different and not merely for the same. That is one reason why societies shaped by Christianity have generally welcomed immigrants, and why the Church itself is the most marvelous illustration of diversity in unity and unity in diversity.

The Church upholds social diversity within the bounds of objectivity and natural law. The Church still believes in rightly ordered ends, hence in cooperating virtues more than in competing "values."

It expects people to give a moral account of their values, not merely to identify and celebrate them. And so it offends pluralists by challenging pluralism as the dominant reality.

Pluralism is a demographic fact. Nothing more, nothing less. It is not a philosophy or ideology. It does not imply that all ideas and religious beliefs are equally valid. The fact that we live in a diverse country requires that we treat each other with respect.

But pluralism does not require us to mute our convictions. Nor does it ever excuse us from speaking and acting to advance our beliefs about justice and the common good in public.

It should also be noted that tolerance is a working principle that enables us to live in peace with each other and their ideas. Most of the time it is a good thing. But it is not an end in itself, and to tolerate or excuse a grave evil in society is itself a grave evil. Christians have a duty not to "tolerate" other people but to love them, which is a much more demanding task. Justice, charity, mercy, courage, prudence—these are Christian virtues; but not tolerance. Real Christian virtues flow from an understanding of truth, unchanging and rooted in God, that exists and obligates us whether we like it or not. The pragmatic social truce we call "tolerance" has no such grounding.

Secularism

Secularism insists that religion must be confined to the private sphere and allowed no direct influence on public life, or on accounts of what belongs to the common good of a particular society.

A liberal democracy, it is said, cannot adhere to a moral tradition that is rooted in religion, even if a majority of its citizens believe that tradition to be more or less sound. It cannot go further in moral matters than to propound tolerance and respect for everyone. If it did go further, it would unfairly restrict the liberty of dissenters and invite social strife between differing traditions.

It is my suspicion that many who say such things are not half so worried about civil strife, which they themselves are not afraid to stir up, or about civil liberties, which they are not afraid to curtail, as about the moral consensus that emerges when religion is not confined to the private sphere.

But let me be clear about the kind of secularism I am talking about. I am not talking about the kind of secularism that Christendom itself generated, the kind that insists on a distinction between Church and State and refuses in principle to allow either to assume the rights and responsibilities of the other.

I am talking about the kind of secularism that arrogates to itself the role that religion once played in binding together the body politic. This is the secularism that, though it denies any public role for religion, is itself a form of religion: a civil religion that obliterates the distinction altogether by making the State both adjudicator and enforcer of the new morality.

Again, let it be said clearly that Christianity has no aversion to the secular. Christianly speaking, "secularity" refers to the ordering of various offices, activities, or objects to the needs of the present age. Embedded in the concept of the secular is a recognition that the present age, while penultimate and strictly provisional, remains worthy of our concern and attention. Yet its affairs should be conducted with a certain modesty. They should not be conducted as if the kingdom of God were definitively established, or could be produced by human efforts, but rather with the humility and sense of accountability that derive from the knowledge that God—having al-

49

ready revealed the King—will Himself produce the kingdom when He brings the present age to an end.

But for those who refuse to acknowledge the King, secularity implies something quite different. It implies liberation from any concern with that which does not belong exclusively to the present age; that is, from everything that concerns the age to come. Consequently it invites utopian enterprises of various kinds: excessive enterprises like communism, fascism and, yes, "human rights" regimes, whose own fascist character is revealed most clearly in their attacks on conscience.

Individualism

To speak of conscience is to come to the third level, where the emphasis falls on the individual. At first glance it may seem odd that conscience should be displaced and even attacked. Conscience, after all, though informed by natural law (the knowledge of which is universal or innate) and by religion (which is learned in community), is a faculty that involves the individual in a dialogue with himself; it belongs to one's self-awareness. So why should those who wish to exalt the individual to the highest place, and to emphasize moral autonomy, make themselves the enemies of conscience?

They do so because the dialogue that conscience demands is not merely a dialogue of the self with itself. It is a dialogue in which the self is questioned, in which the self is called upon to side against itself; that is, to discipline itself by taking up the cause of natural law or of religion. And this is precisely what individualism—the idolatry of the autonomous individual—cannot stand for. Conscience acknowledges autonomy, the freedom of the individual to choose.

But conscience also acknowledges as a correlative the claim of the Creator and of the common good. It asks the self to choose to submit itself to what is higher than itself. For the individualist, however, there is nothing higher than the self. Conscience is therefore the last enemy to be overcome in the battle for the new moral order.

The proponents of this new morality are very shrewd. What better weapon to turn against conscience than human rights? Human rights discourse arose historically on a theological foundation, combining the concerns of natural law, religion, and conscience.

But what if essential elements of that discourse—equality, dignity, autonomy, freedom, etc.—were to be dislocated from their foundation and rearranged as a protective silo against the conscience, so that modern man might get on with his experiments at the edge of morality?

What if the Human Rights Commissions themselves were to declare conscience the real threat to rights, and to prohibit its public manifestation?

Of course, ultimately, this new morality will be enforced by violence.

An illustration of an attempt to impose the new morality— one man's story: Carol Johnson and Norman Greenfield, each, and as far as I can determine independently of one another, filed a complaint with the Alberta Human Rights Commission against the Roman Catholic Diocese of Calgary and myself on the ground of sexual orientation in the area of "goods/services refused and terms of goods/services," and in the area of "publications, notices, signs and statements," based on my January 2005 Pastoral Letter in which I challenged one by one the standard arguments used to support same sex unions as the equivalent of traditional marriage.

It is surprising that the Commission accepted the complaints on the basis of "goods/services refused and terms of goods/services," as there was no explanation as to what constituted the goods or services refused, or their terms. Nor did the complainants set out the manner of discrimination in the areas. In short, although there was no evidence of denial of services as alleged, the Commission proceeded with the complaint.

In the second area, "publications, notices, signs and statements," the evidence was a January 21, 2005 Pastoral Letter signed by myself and issued from the Office of the Catholic Bishop of the Diocese of Calgary.

Since the two complaints were substantially the same, I will spell out the particular of the Greenfield complaint:

The following three statements were alleged to be discriminatory:

a) *"There are also historical, cultural, philosophical, moral and anthropological roots. The failure to attend to the health of all the roots runs the risk of killing the tree and destroying the public good."*

b) *"The principal objective in seeking same-sex "marriage" is not really even about equality rights. The goal is to acquire a powerful psychological weapon to change society's rejection of homosexual activity and lifestyle into gradual, even if reluctant acceptance."*

c) *"Since homosexuality, adultery, prostitution and pornography undermine the foundations of the family, the basis of society, then the State must use its coercive power to proscribe or curtail them in the interests of the common good."*

The letters were published on the website of the Diocese, and republished in the media, "to incite hatred of a person or a class of persons, with the added intention of asking for this same group to be treated with contempt by the Government of Canada and parishioners of the Diocese."

I want to make a few comments on each of these items.

Complaint a) *"There are also historical, cultural, philosophical, moral and anthropological roots. The failure to attend to the health of all the roots runs the risk of killing the tree and destroying the public good."*

This one boggles my mind—where is the discrimination? The full quote is: "The Supreme Court has said that Parliament may redefine marriage, it has not said that it must redefine marriage to include same-sex couples. The Supreme Court Justices talk about reading the Constitution, 'expansively,' and that it is like a 'living tree which by way of progressive interpretation, accommodates and addresses the realities of modern life'."

Nevertheless, I would suggest that there are more roots to the tree than simply the Charter of Rights and Freedom. There are also historical, cultural, philosophical, moral, and anthropological roots. The failure to attend to the health of all the roots runs the risk of killing the tree and destroying the public good.

Complaint b) *"The principal objective in seeking same-sex "marriage" is not really even about equality rights. The goal is to acquire a powerful psychological weapon to change society's rejection of homosexual activity and lifestyle into gradual, even if reluctant acceptance."*

Apparently, a gay activist can make such a statement but I am not permitted to do so.

Writing on August 16, 2000, in the *Chicago Free Press*, homosexual activist Paul Varnell states:

> The fundamental controverted issue about homosexuality is not discrimination, hate crimes or domestic partnerships, but the morality of homosexuality. Even if gays obtain non-discrimination laws, hate crime law and domestic partnership benefits, those can do little to counter the underlying moral condemnation which will continue to fester beneath the law and generate hostility, fuel hate crimes, support conversion therapies, encourage gay youth suicide and inhibit the full social acceptance that is our goal.... So the gay movement, whether we acknowledge it or not, is not a civil rights movement, not even a

sexual liberation movement, but a moral revolution aimed at changing people's view of homosexuality.

Complaint c.1) *"Since homosexuality, adultery, prostitution and pornography undermine the foundations of the family, the basis of society, then the State must use its coercive power to proscribe or curtail them in the interests of the common good."*

Each, in its own way, undermines the foundations of the family. My list was never meant to be exhaustive as the *Catechism of the Catholic Church* also mentions: divorce, fornication, rape, etc.

The state obviously responds to each of these threats to family life in different ways as it exercises its coercive power. The government has a solemn obligation to protect, not re-engineer, an institution that is more fundamental to human life than the state. In a word, it must "build fences" to protect the institution of marriage.

The coercive power of the state extends to traffic laws, tax policy, education curriculum, communication regulations, and a whole host of other areas including marriage.

For example, in the case of marriage, federal legislation prohibits people from marrying if they are related linearly or as brother and sister, whether by whole blood, half blood or by adoption. Specifically: a woman may not marry her grandfather, father, grandson, son or brother. A man may not marry his grandmother, mother, granddaughter, daughter or sister.

The time has come for the government of Canada to use its coercive powers to legislate that a couple being married must be one man and one woman.

Complaint c.2) *"The letters were published on the website of the Diocese, and republished in the media, "to incite hatred of a person or a class of persons, with the added intention of asking for this same group to be treated with contempt by the Government of Canada and parishioners of the Diocese."*

Several times, I have written and stated: "It must be acknowledged that homosexual persons have been and are the object of violent malice in speech or in action. Such treatment deserves condemnation from the Church's pastors wherever it occurs. It reveals a kind of disregard to others which endangers the most fundamental principles of a healthy society. The intrinsic dignity of each person must always be respected in word, in action and in law."

This echoes basic Christian teaching: "they must be accepted with respect, compassion, and sensitivity. Every sign of unjust discrimination in their regard should be avoided (*Catechism of the Catholic Church* [2358]).

The difficult balance is to hold onto both unconditional love and uncompromising truth.

Despite the clarifications presented to the complainants, the Alberta Human Rights Commission and the media, on August 24, 2005, we proceeded to the next stage of the human rights process, Conciliation.

This session is held "without prejudice" so what is said remains in the room and falls under the banner of confidentiality. When asked by the media re what transpired—I said: "Given the nature of my office, the importance of confidentiality, and my own personal reputation, I feel duty bound to adhere to the rules of the process, so I will not comment on what transpired, other than to say I am pleased with the outcome."

Mr. Greenfield had asked me if he could speak to the media after the session. I said, "It's up to you but I'm not going to."

According to Rick Bell of the *Calgary Sun*, Mr. Greenfield said:

What I wanted to do is bring the issue to the media. There really is no other platform to do this, with the media selective in what sort of discussion they want to hear and

55

the lack of public forums in the city for people like myself to go and talk about this issue… I never had a problem with the bishop or what he was preaching from the pulpit. I just had a problem with him asking our provincial government to use their coercive power to make same-sex marriage illegal.

Rick Bell went on to comment that the complaints, taken seriously by the human rights commission, caused substantial stress to Bishop Henry, faithful Christians and freedom lovers across the country, but it does not seem to have entered the equation for Mr. Greenfield or the commission. Moreover, the defense has cost the diocese and its contributors thousands of dollars.

I believe that these complaints were an attempt to intimidate and silence me, the lodging of these complaints constituted a violation of my right of freedom of expression and freedom of religion guaranteed by the Charter of Rights and Freedom, and has revealed a multitude of problems with the Alberta Human Rights Commission and its processes.

These complaints and the process itself were an act of violence seeking to impose the new morality.

Spe Salvi (On Christian Hope)—Benedict XVI:

28. While attending the Sunday liturgy at the port city of Hippo, Augustine was called out from the assembly by the Bishop and constrained to receive ordination for the exercise of the priestly ministry in that city. Looking back on that moment, he writes in his Confessions: "Terrified by my sins and the weight of my misery, I had resolved in my heart, and meditated flight into the wilderness; but you forbade me and gave me strength, by saying: 'Christ died for all, that those who live might live no longer for themselves but for him who for their sake died' (cf. 2

Cor 5:15)" [21]. Christ died for all. To live for him means allowing oneself to be drawn into his being for others.

29. For Augustine this meant a totally new life. He once described his daily life in the following terms: "The turbulent have to be corrected, the faint-hearted cheered up, the weak supported; the Gospel's opponents need to be refuted, its insidious enemies guarded against; the unlearned need to be taught, the indolent stirred up, the argumentative checked; the proud must be put in their place, the desperate set on their feet, those engaged in quarrels reconciled; the needy have to be helped, the oppressed to be liberated, the good to be encouraged, the bad to be tolerated; all must be loved" [22]. "The Gospel terrifies me" [23]—producing that healthy fear which prevents us from living for ourselves alone and compels us to pass on the hope we hold in common. Amid the serious difficulties facing the Roman Empire— and also posing a serious threat to Roman Africa, which was actually destroyed at the end of Augustine's life— this was what he set out to do: to transmit hope, the hope which came to him from faith and which, in complete contrast with his introverted temperament, enabled him to take part decisively and with all his strength in the task of building up the city. In the same chapter of the Confessions in which we have just noted the decisive reason for his commitment "for all," he says that Christ "intercedes for us, otherwise I should despair. My weaknesses are many and grave, many and grave indeed, but more abundant still is your medicine. We might have thought that your word was far distant from union with man, and so we might have despaired of ourselves, if this Word had not become flesh and dwelt among us" [24]. On the strength of his hope, Augustine dedicated

himself completely to the ordinary people and to his city—renouncing his spiritual nobility, he preached and acted in a simple way for simple people.

We too must be men and women of hope who dedicate ourselves completely to the ordinary people and to our cities— renouncing our spiritual nobility, preaching and acting in a simple way for simple people!

A native of London, Ontario, Bishop Frederick Bernard Henry was ordained a priest on May 25, 1968. In 1971, he earned a Master's Degree in Philosophy from the University of Notre Dame, Indiana, and in 1973 a Licentiate in Theology with a Specialization in Fundamental Theology from the Gregorian University in Rome. He was appointed Auxiliary Bishop of London and Titular bishop of Carinola and ordained to the Episcopate on June 24, 1986. He was installed as the fourth Bishop of Thunder Bay on May 11, 1995 and installed as the seventh Bishop of Calgary on March 19, 1998.

Sanctum:
Womb, the Sanctuary of Mercy
Amy C. Schifrin

Octave of the Annunciation, March 2011

In the fall of 1983, I didn't know that there would be over 1.2 million legal abortions performed in North America that year, nor did I know that in 1984 another 1.3 million would also take place.[1] I was newly married, just beginning my senior year at seminary, and nauseated 'round the clock. My husband and I had just traveled to New York and back on a Greyhound bus (we lived in St. Paul, MN), and I had attributed my sensitive stomach to the grease laden food at the truck stops along the way. But now we were settled into our little apartment and ready to do some home cooking and I could barely stand the smell of food. Could it be, would it be, we hoped and prayed and bought a drug-store pregnancy test, whose results were ultimately unclear. Lacking a home physician we made an appointment at the local Planned Parenthood Clinic where I could have a pregnancy test.

---

1. Lilo T. Strauss, M.A., Joy Herndon, M.S., Jeani Chang, M.P.H., Wilda Y. Parker, Sonya V. Bowens, M.S., Suzanne B. Zane, D.V.M., Cynthia J. Berg, M.D., *Division of Reproductive Health National Center for Chronic Disease Prevention and Health Promotion*, "Abortion Surveillance—United States, 2001," CDC/National Center for Chronic Disease Prevention and Health Promotion/Division of Reproductive Health. http://www.cdc.gov/mmwr/preview/mmwrhtml/ss5309a1.htm.

Sitting together in the waiting room anxious for the results, a healthcare worker called me in and said that my husband would have to stay in the waiting room. I didn't understand, couldn't he come in with me? No, she said, they wanted to talk to me alone first. I didn't understand. Even more anxious and worried that something was terribly wrong with me, I was finally given the news that I was pregnant. Overjoyed, I wanted my husband to hear, and that's when I found out from Planned Parenthood that they always tell the mother alone first in case she does not want to continue the pregnancy. In fact, she was surprised that I did, for I had been the first woman in many weeks for whom the news was heard as good news.

Word spread like wildfire among the doctors, nurses, and technicians, who then treated us like royalty. Even those who dealt in death, could yet be surprised by life, and in that moment, our joy was contagious. I can only hope that in some small way it had a lasting effect to help turn their hearts to life.

As we are gathered in on this Octave of Annunciation by the Good News given to Mary, Most Holy *Theotokos*, we come to know the gift of every life in a new way, and we come to know the holiness and sacredness of the womb as a sanctuary of mercy for all humankind. She who is our mother in the faith shelters the One who is the Saviour of the world with her very body, with her very womanhood. She gives her life for another, a model of trust beyond all fear, a model of obedience beyond all personal security, a model of faith in the One who is yet unseen, until the glorious day of His birth, when she revels in His radiant face at her breast.

In the kenotic movement of God in the incarnation, He was never more vulnerable, more helpless then when He was *in utero*, swaddled in amniotic fluid, yet He was also never more intimately protected, swaddled in the myriad layers of a mother's love. And it is the vision of this love that is ever so needed, a death defying love, an eternal love, a fierce love, a sacrificing love, that we are called to bear for the sake of generations to come. For in the disordered loving of a fallen world that removes sexual intercourse from the fidelity and delight of the marriage bed, there will continue to be the littlest among us, made in the image and likeness of God, who without such love, will be unprotected from the lies that say they are neither human or of any value.

If, as St. Paul teaches us, faith comes by hearing (Romans 10:17), then we need to sing to all the world as the angel did for Mary, so that the anti-Gospel of self-determination, self-liberation, and self-exaltation (an un-holy trinity…) will not be the last word that any man or woman hears in the landscape of a time when abortion is legal, and civically, considered moral. From the moment of conception our Lord is fully human and fully divine,[2] veiled in Mary's flesh, His protector, His sanctuary. From the moment of conception, we are indeed who we are as well.[3] It is only our relationship to others that will take on new dimensions as we grow into the world, for our humanity is fully present (i.e., all that is needed for faith has

---

2. Council of Chalcedon (451 A.D.) "We confess the Holy Virgin to be the Mother of God because God the Word was made flesh and became man from the moment of conception." See also Formula of Concord, Epitome, Article VII.10, "Therefore we believe, teach, and confess that the Son of man according to his human nature is really (that is, in deed and in truth) exalted to the right hand of the omnipotent majesty and power of God, because he was assumed into God when he was conceived by the Holy Spirit in his mother's womb and his human nature was personally united with the Son of the Most High." *Book of Concord: The Confessions of the Evangelical Lutheran Church*, trans. and ed. Theodore Tappert (Philadelphia: Fortress Press, 1959), 488.

3. "Our particular concern here is what is the being and nature of the unborn child as a besouled body or an embodied soul from the very beginning of existence in the womb of the mother. The unborn child is already a human being in germ,' as it were…That is to say, the human being is already genetically complete in the womb from the moment of conception, when the body and soul of the new human being grow together in the womb of the mother and in living relation to her. The human genome thus come into being is laden by the Creator with all the information that is needed for development." Thomas F. Torrence, "The Being and Nature of the Unborn Child," *Theology Matters*, vol 6, no 4 (Jul/Aug 2000): 2.

been given us as we have no choice but to depend upon another for life). And if the glory of God is man fully alive,[4] then the rapid multiplication of your cells is as glorious as a Bach Cantata!

What if every woman with a child in her womb was to hear the angel's words, "The Lord is with you"? The Lord is with you in this pregnancy whether you loved your husband or not, whether you had a husband or not. The Lord is with you, whether this child was conceived in love or whether you suffered through a horrific rape. The Lord is with you whether you were trolling for anonymous sex in a seedy bar or whether you were looking for comfort in all the wrong places. The Lord is with you whether your father sold you to this brute or whether your own father was the brute. Whatever unspeakable shame was done is not the last word because the Lord is with you and with your little one. The Lord is suffering with you and the Lord will lead you to that day when He will be rejoicing with you. In this pregnancy, however un-timed or un-planned, the Lord is with you, because no life is made without Him. As Luther's *Small Catechism* attests, "I believe that God has created me and all that exists."[5]

With few exceptions, until the mid-twentieth century the church's witness through the ages has clearly proclaimed to all who would hear that every child created has his/her origins in the love of God for the world He has created. While in our rebellion against His sovereignty we have not lived out His intentions for us, He has not given up on us, creating new life generation after generation. The testimony of the early church was clear: The *Didache* speaks of those who seek to end the life of one *in utero* as "killers of the child, who abort the mold of God."[6] The Epistle of Barnabus speaks,

---

4. St. Irenaeus.

5. *Book of Concord: The Confessions of the Evangelical Lutheran Church*, trans. and ed. Theodore Tappert (Philadelphia: Fortress Press, 1959), 345.

6. *Didache* 2:2

"Thou shalt not murder a child by abortion, nor again shalt thou kill it when it is born."[7] St. Basil the Great clearly proclaims that one's passage through the birth canal does not mark the beginning of life, calling men who arrange for the abortions of their illegitimate children "worse than murderers," because not only have they murdered the child, they have made the prostitute mother into a murderer as well.[8] I find St. Basil's word especially revealing when speaking to women who talk about legalized abortion giving them the freedom of choice, for 'abortion on demand' gives women the freedom to have sex with men who think of them as no better than receptacles—truly de-humanized objects. It gives women the freedom to have sex with men who care more about their own gratification than the needs, concerns, or desires of anyone else. It gives women the freedom to have sex with men who won't remember their name tomorrow, and for whom sex is not only disassociated with pro-creation, it is disassociated with any understanding that sexual intercourse is the union of two *human beings*. Not only is the child thought of as less than human, so is the mother. And as Blessed St. Dietrich Bonhoeffer reminds us, it is union, even more than pro-creation, that serves as a foundation of marriage.[9] Men and women who engage in sexual intercourse to simply gratify a bodily urge without regard to the life of their momentary partner, i.e., they treat their partner as an object devoid of the human spirit, can easily project that same split to a child *in utero*. St. Augustine and St. Thomas Aquinas, following the rationale of Aristotle, would propose that there is a certain point in the fetus' development where a soul enters, but such argumentation is clearly in disagreement with the consensus of witnesses throughout the first millennium of

---

7. *The Epistle of Barnabas* 19:5

8. *Abortion: What Does the Church Teach? The Orthodox Perspective on Abortion, as Presented to the United States Supreme Court in THE AMICUS CURIAE* (*Friend of the Court*), *BRIEF* (Ben Lomomd, CA: Conciliar Press, 1989): 7.

9. Dietrich Bonhoeffer, *Ethics* (New York: Macmillian, 1965): 179.

Christendom and beyond.[10] As St. Gregory of Nyssa (c.335-394) writes, "There is no question about that which is bred in the uterus, both growing, and moving from place to place. It remains, therefore, that we must think that the point of commencement of existence is one and the same for body and soul."[11]

When legalized abortion is used as a retroactive means of birth control, or as the antidote for "recreational sex," everyone is diminished.[12] The man, because he is not open to receiving what the woman, as a full human being, has to give him as a full human being: what he could learn from her in a relationship in which spirituality and sexuality are not divorced, what he could learn about being a man as he cares for his children, and what he could learn about the goodness of God who has given him someone to love him enough that she would invite him into her own body. The woman,

---

10. Roe v. Wade attempts to show that "Abortion was philosophically and morally grounded in Judeo-Christian tradition. To the extent such perception is the foundation of Roe, the Orthodox Church bears an undivided witness to the fact that it is a perception which is utterly inconsistent with the experience of historic Christianity…. The Church's teaching represented a significant departure from Aristotelian thought, and from the beginning regarded abortion as abhorrent and an abomination before God." *Abortion: What Does the Church Teach?*, 5-6.

11. *Abortion: What Does the Church Teach?*, 8.

12. The easy availability of legal abortion is only "necessary" when it is indeed used as birth control. Now that it is legal, pro-abortionists are not afraid to uphold this practice. Abortion Rights Coalition of Canada (*ARCC*) literature states that, "It's only in the last 50 years or so that women, at least in the western world, have really achieved the means to control their own fertility. Many reliable methods of contraception exist to choose from, and when all else fails, we now have legal and safe abortion. Abortion is a crucial backstop for contraception, it's the birth control method of last resort. It's impossible for women to really control their fertility without access to abortion because no contraceptive is 100% effective, and because women can't always access birth control or may not use it correctly." Joyce Arthur, "Paternity, Patriarchy, and Reproductive Rights," Speech given 12/2/06 at the Remember me" memorial in Vancouver, BC, http://www.arcc-cdac.ca/action/paternity.html.

who even in this femininely sexually aggressive culture, would have to live in a perpetual state of denial that God made her in such a way that love and sexual expression cannot be rent asunder without doing damage to her primary identity and who would never know the joy of giving thanks to God for being gifted with the exquisite beauty and mighty strength of a womb, and who could never look at another child without regret. The man and woman together, whose mutual fulfillment and complementarity as an eschatological sign of God's intentions for Christ and His church will have vanished. And the child, the blessed and innocent child, no mere lump of tissue, but a living human presence, who even hidden in secret is the apple of God's eye, the work of His hands, the delight of His heart, who is denied the fullness of body that was intended for him in this life and in the age to come, for it is bodies that will be resurrected. Everyone is diminished. Everyone loses.

It is then no surprise that in a day and an age when the revisionist church's hermeneutic of suspicion trumps the Apostolic witness and it fails to preach bodily resurrection, that it also fails to proclaim the sanctity of all human life, for the two are intricately intertwined. When a church acts as if it no longer believes that the resurrected Christ's body is truly present at the altar, it would have no reason to believe that He is fully present as Lord in the tabernacle of his mother's body.[13] And if a church does not believe that He who is the Saviour of the world is fully human and fully divine from the moment of His conception, it would have no way to understand that there is a sacramentality to our bodies, to our lives, as the enfleshment of His divine love. God did not create us apart from our bodies, nor will He resurrect us apart from them. God

---

13. "The Blessed Virgin Mary was the first human person who could say of Jesus, "This is my body, this is my blood." She was the first altar of the Incarnation's mystery. Her body a fitting temple, she was the prime analogate for those who know and live the mysteries of transubstantiation." John F. Kavanaugh, "This Is My Body," *America*, 169, Issue 19: 23.

creates us in these bodies that we may live.[14] For it is in a body that life is experienced. It is in a body that we see the world around us. It is in a body that we hear our names. It is in a body that we feel pain when we are cut or bruised. It is in a body that terror smells as foul as sweat. It is in a body that delight glimmers as a smile. It is in a body that the pressure of a hand's touch tells more about a person's heart then their words might ever reveal. It is in a body, as St. Paul preaches, that we will groan for redemption (Romans 8:22). Real presence does not evaporate because the world looks the other way.

The abortion industry has worked hard to convince us that life is not a good gift from a good God.[15] For them, the earth is *not* the Lord's and its fullness thereof. The flowering of this industry and its ideology in the 21st century is the fruit of an anti-theology void of sacramentality. And as with many social issues, it has gained purchase because it has cast itself as part of a justice issue, and like many such arguments it begins with the simple and moves to the complex. People nod their assent to a series of truisms or generalities, until, before they know it, they are caught in an ever-tightening web. This is how it goes: Men have had a power that woman have not had. All one has to do is read a classic history book or check the statistics on pay scales for men and women who work at the same jobs. You can look at the pay differentials for careers that have traditionally

---

14. "Our God is the God who gives life instead of the death of the world. Right there, it seems to me, is the most radical contradiction to abortion—that God desires that all persons, whom he has created, live and not die. And surely the child in the womb is included in that number... We clever human beings may fertilize human eggs in a petri dish and even clone ourselves, but God furnished the initial cells and the DNA, and apart from his creation of life, our science would be impossible. We come from God, and his purpose for all of us—born and unborn—is that we live." Elizabeth Achtemeier, "Abortion and the Sacraments," *Theology Matters* 5, no 3 (May/June 1999): 2.

15. For a comprehensive study on the change in the Christian community's attitudes towards abortions and societal influences see, Mark G. Toulouse, "Perspectives on Abortion in the Christian Community from the 1950s to the Early 1990s," *Encounter* 63, no 4 (Autumn 2001): 327-403.

belonged to women and see of how much less monetary value they are as compared to those which have traditionally been associated with men. Upper body strength aside, pregnancy and the potential need for maternity leave and care of children are where crucial differences lie.[16] If the playing field was equitable and just, and women could continue in their self-determined and commercial worth, well then, the society might value them as much as it values men. And then indeed women would be able to live as "freely" as men in all aspects of their lives from the economic to the sexual. Who can argue against that? Aren't men and women equal? Access to legal abortion is critical for such equality.[17]

Here is an example of such an argument in classic form from the *Pro-choice Action Network of Canada*[18] presented in an essay entitled, "Legal Abortion: the Sign of a Civilized Society."

---

16. Pro-abortion activists will blame all the world's ills on this differentiation of the sexes. "…in my view, the biggest difference by far between men and women, the only one that's really important – is that women can bear children and men cannot. I think that difference, in one way or another, directly or indirectly, accounts for virtually all the oppression and violence against women we see in the world today." Joyce Arthur, "Paternity, Patriarchy, and Reproductive Rights," Speech given 12/2/06 at the Remember me" memorial in Vancouver, BC, http://www.arcc-cdac.ca/action/paternity.html.

17. Elizabeth Achtemeier clearly posits the opposing Christian view, "…the siren song of our society is very strong: women should be able to maintain control over their bodies and personal lives; lifestyles, education, future plans should be undisturbed and left in comfort; the weak and helpless can be sacrificed to the able; there are some who will never contribute to the material wealth of the nation or who will cost it money, and who therefore should be eliminated. Control, comfort, ability, wealth—these characterize the goals of our society and prop up the demands for abortion rights. And every one of them contradicts the unique life asked of Christians, for Christians are called to turn over control of their lives to God in Jesus Christ and to look for all their ability and welfare from their Lord." Elizabeth Achtemeier, "Abortion and the Sacraments," *Theology Matters* 5, no. 3 (May/June 1999): 2.

18. *Pro-choice Action Network* was subsumed under the *Abortion Rights Coalition of Canada (ARCC)* in 2005.

The process of becoming civilized is a long and painful one. 10,000 years ago, we lived short, brutish lives in caves. Although we soon advanced to huts and houses — and palaces for the privileged few — our lives largely remained short and brutish. Here and there over the past 2,000 years, ordinary people were deemed to have some rights, too, not just kings, popes, and emperors. At first, these rights extended only to men, or to landowners, or to those of the right colour or heritage... Only 73 years ago, the world officially condemned slavery. The enlightened recognition that enslaving people was evil made it possible to actually try and stop it... Mandatory motherhood is a unique kind of slavery that specifically victimizes women and children. About one-third of the world's women live in countries where enforced motherhood rules the day. Not too long ago, perhaps women's biology was their destiny. But no more. With the advent of modern contraception and quality reproductive care, there's no excuse for forcing women to bear children against their will, or failing to provide basic maternal care, or compelling women to seek out illegal, unsafe abortions...

Then after recounting the numerous health risks of childbirth and the relative safety and ease of abortion the essay shows its true colours:

When women can control their reproduction, it leaves them free to pursue higher education and careers, and to plan their lives and families. Women should not be expected to sacrifice their personal and economic freedom to have babies they don't want.[19]

The pro-abortionist argument has changed through the years, and the legalization and social acceptability of abortion is at the

19. Joyce Arthur, "Legal Abortion: A Sign of a Civilized Society," c. October, 1999, http://www.prochoiceactionnetwork-canada.org/civilize.html.

crux of the presentation of the ever-developing argument. When Margaret Sanger and her cohorts formed the American Birth Control Federation of America, the forerunner of Planned Parenthood in the early 20th century, this "justice" issue was framed in terms of care for the poor and the lessening of the burden of the underclass on the general society. Then the rationale that existed 50 years ago, just before Roe v. Wade, when young unmarried pregnant women were still banished, was about removing the shroud of shame that colored a woman's life or about how illegal abortions brought about death for poor women, but that rich (rich white) women could always find a clean surgeon's knife. As the issue of societal and cultural shame diminished for unwed mothers, newer arguments were framed, arguments that would not be necessary if abortion were not a widespread legal practice and especially an expectation in the North American context for women who do not want to bear the child with whom they are pregnant. Threads of the earlier argument remain but when abortion is a legal entity a different "justice" argument must be made in the face of those who seek to expose the fallacy of these presuppositions. The justice issue now is about the rights of the mother over the rights of the fetus, or even of the father. Again, it is precisely the opposite of what St. Paul has to say, "Present your bodies as a living sacrifice" (Romans 12:1). As the *Abortion Rights Coalition of Canada (ARCC)* teaches, "focusing on the fetus always has dire legal and social consequences for women, and devalues women," and "true justice demands that women not be compelled to bear children they don't want."[20] As we can once again clearly see, human justice is never quite God's justice. The lack of focus on the fetus and the absence of any language that speaks of either the embryo or fetus as a life in relationship to his

---

20. Joyce Arthur, "How to Think about the Fetus," http://www.arcc-cdac.ca/presentations/fetusposter.pdf. *NARAL (National Abortion Rights Action League) Pro-Choice America* calls the blocking of federally-funded abortion coverage in current House bill H.R. 3 another front in the "War against Women." http://www.prochoiceamerica.org/media/press-releases/2011/pr03032011_hr3.html.

or her mother is standard in Planned Parenthood propagandizing material. Depending upon how advanced a woman's pregnancy is, she can have either a medication (i.e. drug induced) abortion or a surgical one. The instruction video explaining a medication abortion speaks about the abortion feeling more natural, as if the woman were experiencing a miscarriage, which she may now experience in the privacy of her own home, and if she wants no one else to know, she is left to feel the pain alone.[21]

Currently, in the United States, approximately one out of three women between the ages of 22 and 45 has had a legal abortion.[22] Included in this group are not only young single poor women or women for whom the aborting of their children was considered the only means available to save their lives, but married women, educated women, working women.[23] 40% of women between the ages of 40 and 55 in the U.S. have had abortions.[24] Following Roe v. Wade in the U.S. and the Morganthaler Law in Canada, the rationales for having an abortion multiply. This is yet another example of how we make the law (or seek justice) in our image and likeness when there is no external (i.e. divine) standard. Again, the

---

21. http://www.plannedparenthood.org/health-topics/abortion/abortion-pill-medication-abortion-4354.asp

22. Johnston, W. R., 4 June 2008, "Historical abortion statistics: United States," on line, Johnston's Archive, http://www.johnstonsarchive.net/policy/abortion/uslifetimeab.html . See also Alan Guttmacher Institute, Jan. 2008, "An overview of abortion in the United States," *Guttmacher Institute*, on line http://www.guttmacher.org/media/presskits/2005/06/28/abortionoverview.html

23. Ironically and tragically, as the availability of early sonograms and legalized abortion spread throughout the world, female fetuses are being aborted at alarming rates. The issue of sex selection as a basis for abortion will hold unforeseen consequences for the global community. See Joe Carter, "The Global War Against Baby Girls," *First Things: On the Square*, March 16, 2011. http://www.firstthings.com/onthesquare/2011/03/the-global-war-against-baby-girls

24. Johnston, W. R., 4 June 2008, "Historical abortion statistics: United States," on line, *Johnston's Archive*, http://www.johnstonsarchive.net/policy/abortion/uslifetimeab.html

ARCC now teaches, "women have the right to abortion even if the fetus is a legal person with rights, because a pregnant woman has the right to defend life and health with an abortion," and most damning of all, "the pregnant woman's opinion is the only one that counts. A fetus becomes a person when the woman carrying it decides it does."[25] The creation of life is no longer considered as God's domain, but only the human's.

An extreme form of the pro-abortionist's argument posits that abortion is a form of self-defense against the invading fetus. With legalized abortion, they state that there is a higher risk of death for mothers during childbirth than there is during a legal abortion, and since no mother is under obligation to donate an organ or even blood to save a child's life, neither is she under any obligation to risk her life for an unwanted child. *ARCC* states, "A fetus is not 'innocent' ... [for] it is co-opting the woman's body and endangering her health against her will...The woman has a right to defend herself with an abortion."[26] Because modern medicine has given us a glorious view into the expectant womb, it becomes harder and harder to deny that there is life in there, so they try to move their rationale away from the discussion of the rights or life of the growing fetus.[27] Part of their goal is to move the question of when does life begin to the realm of opinion, to something which cannot be known in fact, but which is purely subjective. Because recent medical advances have given us the ability to view life in the womb as well as given us the ability to sustain early pre-term babies, abortionists have had to change the basis of their argument. For while a secular

25. Joyce Arthur, "How to Think about the Fetus," http://www.arcc-cdac.ca/presentations/fetusposter.pdf . See also Joyce Arthur, "The Fetus Focus Fallacy," *Pro-Choice Press*, Spring 2005, http://www.prochoiceactionnetwork-canada.org/articles/fetus-focus-fallacy.shtml

26. Joyce Arthur, "How to Think about the Fetus," http://www.arcc-cdac.ca/presentations/fetusposter.pdf .

27. Eileen L. McDonagh, "Adding Consent to Choice in the Abortion Debate," *Society* 42, no. 5. (July/August 2005): 18-26.

society may never agree on when life "becomes" sacred, or even when life becomes viable, there is simply scientific evidence of life, real life, of a human person, in the tiniest form, so beautiful that all we can do is grab a sharp intake of air, now speechless with awe. Instead of denying that this little one is a person with rights, they move the argument to speak of how the presence of a fetus, even if it has rights, does not supersede the rights of the mother. If there ever was an anti-Marian theology, this is it. "Let it be to me according to your will" is not part of the pro-choice vocabulary, a vocabulary in which the self believes it is God. In "The Fetus Focus Fallacy," Joyce Arthur of *ARCC* writes about her own abortion experience,

> The thing that enraged me then, and still does today, is this single overriding thought: *How dare they*. How dare anyone tell me what I can do with my body, my life… Ultimately, I am the final arbiter when it comes to my life. And my decision-making ability includes deciding the fate of my embryo or fetus. Since it lives inside my body and is completely dependent on me and no-one else for its survival, it literally belongs to me and no-one else."[28]

Among the many things she misses, including the sovereignty of God and the faith that every child belongs first to God, is that now the fetus is a slave to her whims, since she clearly states that the woman has de-humanized the child to an *it*. *It* is property that belongs to her, and she has the right to grant life or terminate it.

With the expansion of such an ideology, what was done in dire circumstances is now a fact for one-third of the female population and by extension for the males who impregnated them. We see the fall from Eden with a glaring clarity, as one sin compounds into another. Denial becomes a collective expression of anesthesia, for if, as psychologists have long reported, the death of a child

---

28. Joyce Arthur, "The Fetus Focus Fallacy," *Pro-Choice Press*, Spring 2005, http://www.prochoiceactionnetwork-canada.org/articles/fetus-focus-fallacy.shtml.

is the deepest grief that anyone can experience, then the minimization that this little one in the womb is not truly a child of great value must be repeated at every opportunity. As one of the cornerstones of the abortion industry's propaganda, it must be maintained at all costs. What happens to a woman who has undergone an abortion and a few years later "happily" finds herself pregnant? Now, once the pregnancy is confirmed, she receives prenatal vitamins and specialized care. She sees pictures of the embryo and then fetus in development, she hears a heartbeat at her doctor's office, she eats for two, she feels that first kick. Will her denial break down, that the one whom she aborted was more than mere inconvenience or just some unformed tissue? Will she try to come up with a rationale depending upon in what week of her pregnancy the abortion took place? Or will the new life in her speak with such clarity through his or her presence, that she can no longer deny that this indeed is life?

A fetus (young one/offspring), in the third month of his or her development *in utero*, in addition to having use of her arms or sucking his thumb, has fully developed vocal chords—the ability to cry out. It is only the absence of air in that sea of amniotic fluid that keeps such sound from coming to fruition in our ears. A percentage of abortions that are performed in the U.S. and Canada are in women who have already born a child but who don't want one more at that particular time. How great must their denial become in order to suppress the sound of their aborted child's cry? How much greater will their shame be if anyone were to find out? Greater than that of the pregnant teenager? Abortion has not made life better for them in terms of their relationship with God and neighbor, for while it may have given them an opportunity for temporary economic stability or advancement, or it may have helped them exit an abusive relationship, it has not given them the means to live their lives in the peace that comes from trusting that God is the author and giver of life. If this now aborted life wasn't God's child, then any faith that their own life was, has disappeared. And living life apart from such faith is a living death, for living as if everything depended on them rather than on God is a heavier burden, a tighter yoke than they could have imagined. If they don't buy into the pro-abortion culture of denial, they will be faced with the magnitude of their sin, which can only come to an end when it is laid at the foot of the cross. They, in particular, need a vision of Mary: thirteen, poor, on the edge of being dismissed from her betrothed, sheltering in her rounded womb One who would have made her unmarriageable to anyone else, One by whom no earthy gain could be had, One whom she would know from the start was more than her creation, One whom she would adore, One whose suffering and death would pierce her soul. With love, there is always the possibility of grief and death, sorrow and loss. With love, there is always the possibility of healing. With love that trusts God so as to place the life of another above one's own life, there is always hope, (i.e., suffering, endurance, character, and hope) hope that causes us to move within His will (Romans 5:3-5).

There is no doubt that men, hell bent on their own way, have raped women in and out of marriage. They have pillaged and destroyed lives in a physical expression of earthly conquest. There is no doubt that they have defied God when they visited prostitutes, seduced young girls, or taken their sisters and daughters to their beds. There is no doubt that somewhere in every family history on earth there is a life that was the product of rape. Having women act like men when they are behaving at their worst is not the answer, in fact it will only perpetuate the problem. There will be no need for the man to change his rough and violent ways if abortion is an acceptable "final solution" to an inconvenient or inopportune conception. (This has been recently documented by the undercover work of Live Action, which shows how easy it is for a pimp to arrange an abortion at Planned Parenthood for an underage girl so that she can go back to work as a prostitute.[29])

---

29. Lila Rose, President of Live Action, http://www.watchglennbeck.com/video/2011/february/glenn-beck-show-february-18-2011-planned-parenthood-exposed/

The woman who aborts is no greater sinner than the man who impregnates a woman who is not his wife. (Mt 5:21-22; 27-28) She has simply become like the man whom she despises, the man who has treated her as less than human. Ironically, it is she, not he, who will be undergoing the surgeon's knife in an abortion. But in addition to losing the child and losing a piece of her humanity, she is losing what it means to have been chosen by God to have a womb, for of all the gifts with which He endows us is there anything greater than His entrusting to her the sacred place in which to care for another in her very body? How He must love her to have created her with such capacities. How He must love her to have created her to bear His most sacred possessions, His children. How He must love her, for it is by a woman that He will choose to enter the world in a way that we could at last know Him. When the angel tells Mary she will conceive and bear a son we learn that He who will grow in her womb will share all of what it means to be human with us, even nine months *in utero*.

Those nine months, those holy months in which Mary sings of what God has done for her, are remembered for our sake in the church's witness through the liturgical year. Those months are remembered, because those are the number of our months, too, and because the one who comes to life in Mary's womb spends those nine months there for each of us. Nine months between March 25 and December 25, nine months between conception and breath, nine months between an angel's whisper and the heavens so full of glory that not one angel could keep silent. On March 25 our hope begins, for on March 25 the world turns on its axis, for just when day and night are divided at the vernal equinox, just as the lambs are being prepared for the Passover (Nisan 14 on the lunar calendar), just when the Jews are recounting the mighty acts of God, the name of our Saviour is sung into a Virgin's ear. It is an annunciation for all the world to hear. All men and women who seek to use their bodies faithfully need to lean towards the sound of Gabriel's voice until they, too, arrive at Mary's heart. She will lead them to Jesus, for her body is the sanctuary in which He dwells, her womb is the place of mercy incarnate, and in the witness of her trust, she will help them to see the greatness of God's love for them and for their children.

When I left my first call in Canada and moved back to the States I learned an odd form, a terrible form of what could only be called situation ethics. (Abortion was not yet legal in Canada, but was in the U.S.) The scenario went something like this: I would never have an abortion, but since I can't walk in your shoes (or sleep in your bed or live in your family relationships), I can't tell you what to do. There are many options, and the church documents which speak of abortion as a "tragic option /last resort" were ever before me. Even if I were to say that abortion were wrong for me in any circumstance, since it was a legal option I had learned that I had no right to make the determination for you about what path you should pursue. I could ask the woman (and it was always a woman who came to talk to me, never a man and woman together) what she thought her options were, and they would always fall roughly into four categories: 1. Have the baby and live as a single parent; 2. Marry the father if she who knew who the father was and he wasn't a dangerous or abusive man, or wasn't already married; 3. Adoption, giving the baby a chance to grow in love in a stable and secure family; and 4. Abortion, the end of the pregnancy. I could have a conversation about the outcomes of all four categories, but I had learned from my pastoral colleagues and from my wider denominational community to stop short at leading the woman to a decision.

After making the case in a generic way for one of the first three options, I would simply let her know that with whatever option she chose, she would have pain, and I would continue to walk with her in her pain and help her find the immediate resources she needed if she were to keep the baby. I also let her know that were she to bear this child, she would have joy, albeit in the midst of pain, but she would have joy. My concern in that moment was to keep her relationship with the church open and active, because almost every woman who came to see me came with her head bowed and heart filled with disgrace.

But somewhere along the way, I lost that post-modern spirit of pastoral "neutrality" for I realized that if the woman chose Option 4 she would be choosing death, a literal death for her child, a spiritual and existential death for herself and maybe also for her baby's father. Were she to seek an abortion she would be guilty of a great sin, but so would the constellation of people who had a part in shaping her path—a father or uncle or teacher or friend of the family who first sexually abused her, a mother who sided with a stepfather after he had abused her, a boy who date-raped her. When I trained as a chaplain in a juvenile chemical dependency unit, I met 13 and 14 year old girls who would go drinking with groups of boys, naively wanting some male attention, and then when the girl was incapacitated and inebriated each boy would have his sexual turn with her. Some of these 14 year old girls had had sexual intercourse with more than a hundred boys, and not once did any of them describe receiving any sexual pleasure from those encounters, just pain and shame, which they would try to hide in an alcoholic obliteration.

It took me a long time to know how to speak to a young woman in such a way that she could see her own complicity in the sin (remember St. Basil and the prostitute who has now become a murderer), without placing the weight of everyone else's sin on her shoulders. That didn't happen until I started hearing the experiences and finally the confessions of women who had had abortions ten or twenty or even thirty years earlier, who were still in pain until they left it in confession at the cross. Still in pain until they were embraced by the love of the Resurrected One. And from the testimony of those women I finally returned to the Apostolic witness and truly learned to speak of the love that is greater than sin.

For with my eyes now opened I could see that Option 4 (abortion) was no option at all as it was the only one that would lead to more pain because it involved the death of another. Regardless of whether or not the woman had been a willing participant in the conception, this pain would simply go on, either actively or in the form of denial.

When I look at the evolution of the social statements from the ELCA and ELCIC and their predecessor bodies I can now see where the persuasion began. (The church bodies were being reflective of the prevailing society which approved of "therapeutic abortion" and which gradually moved and found more and more reasons that could be included under therapeutic.[30]) There is a point where the statements move from the declaration that abortion is an option only to save the life of the mother to stating that there is no consensus,[31] which leaves the individual with the ultimate decision.[32] What happens then is just what I mistakenly did, for in announcing that there is no consensus, we are collectively saying that all sorts of behaviors are acceptable. The decision about abortion becomes not only personal, but privatized. No one else can validly comment when human experience is privileged over Apostolic witness. What is missing from the church's social statements is any sense that the full humanity of Jesus, the sacramentality of His life even *in utero*, and the witness of Mary is where the discussion should start. And when a discussion starts at the wrong place it is more often than not likely to end in the wrong place. At the root of the social statements is an ethics based on the current cultural and legal situation, masked in a generic concept of love and a myopically human concept of justice, not one that is divine.

---

30. Mark G. Toulous, "Perspectives on Abortion in the Christian Community from the 1950s to the Early 1990's," *Encounter* 62, no 4 Aut 2001: 342-343.

31. http://www.elca.org/What-We-Believe/Social-Issues/Journal-of-Lutheran-Ethics/Portfolios/Social-Statements-of-the-ELCA/Predecessor-Church-Body-Documents/American-Lutheran-Church/Abortion-A-Statement-of-The-American-Lutheran-Church-1976.aspx; http://www.elca.org/What-We-Believe/Social-Issues/Social-Statements/Abortion.aspx.

32. Shades of ELCA CWA 2009, where there is also "no consensus," so that anything becomes acceptable.

What happens to a woman who has had an abortion and then seeks to talk to a pastor when she is overcome with sorrow, guilt, or despair? If the pastor understands abortion to be a morally acceptable option, the woman's confession and repentance will not be answered with absolution.[33] She will be denied the forgiveness of sin that she so desperately needs in order to begin anew, and her misery will lead to some inwardly or outwardly destructive expression. The pastor, unwittingly, and even the denomination are then extensions of an abortion industry in which during the era between 1980 and 2000, 99.3% of legal abortions performed were for non-therapeutic reasons.[34]

Our silence becomes consent to continued fracturing of the family through the misuse of the good gift of sexuality. The woman did not become pregnant alone, so there is at least a community of two whom God intends to use to care for every child conceived. Men and women are called to guard the life of every child in the womb, just as Joseph did in sheltering a pregnant Mary. Joseph becomes a participant in the life of Jesus as the guardian, a true model of manhood, so that Mary can be the mother she was intended to be. As the Liturgy of St. Basil sings, "From you, God took flesh

---

33. "When the Church bases its morality in circumstances rather than the Law, it puts human beings in peril, both physically and spiritually. When a young woman enters an abortion clinic and finds an attractive religious brochure with her denomination's name on it, sanctioning her abortion decision, the defenses of her own troubled conscience are broken down. The church has abetted her spiritual peril. When the Church then denies her need for forgiveness by regarding abortion as morally equivalent to preserving innocent human life, it has set up a barrier to her healing and reconciliation with God." Terry Schlossberg, "The Duties of Love: A Christian Response to Abortion," *Theology Matters* (May/June 2005): 13.

34. "1,506,770, or 99.3%, of the annual number of 1,517,290 abortions from 1980 through 2000 were 'lifestyle,' or non-therapeutic abortions. (Therapeutic abortions include the 'hard cases,' abortions performed when the mother's life or health is at risk, when the pregnancy resulted from rape or incest and when testing predicts fetal birth defects.)" Marybeth T. Hagen, *Abortion: A Mother's Plea for Maternity and the Unborn* (Ligouri, Missouri: Ligouri/Triumph Press, 2005): 55.

and became a little child, He, who is from eternity our God. Your womb, He took as throne. Your body, He made wider than the heavens."[35] Your body, He made wider than the heavens—The Lord is with her, so that He may be with all of us, from our conception unto eternal life. *Sanctum, Sanctum Sanctorum:* In the mystery of God's will, her womb surrounds the only Son of the Father from eternity. *Sanctum:* In the mystery of God's will our wombs are His sanctuary of mercy for all the world.

Amy C. Schifrin, Ph.D., STS, was born in Queens, New York, and studied music at Arizona State University (B.Mus.) and Northwestern University (M.Mus.) Ordained into the ELCC in 1984, she received her M.Div. from Luther-Northwestern Theological Seminary and later, her Ph.D in Liturgical Studies and Homiletics from the Graduate Theological Union. She has served in parish, university, and seminary ministries in both Canada and the U.S., and is currently serving as an interim pastor in Harrisburg, Pennsylvania. She is the author of several books and numerous articles in liturgical and ritual studies, and is the happy mother of two grown sons, Hans and Nils Tolpingrud.

---

35. Liturgy of St. Basil.

Marriage and the Moral Order

Patrick Henry Reardon

Whatever its merits as a tool of historical reconstruction, the classical Documentary Hypothesis was of precious little help in the actual exegesis of the Pentateuch. Whether or not the Jahvist or the Elohist actually existed, we young students of the Bible were taught—half a century ago—how to identify them as underlying literary sources that had been incorporated into Exodus, Numbers, or whatever.

I gave up the exercise about thirty years ago, when I noticed how the Hypothesis was cramping my biblical vision. In spite of all the modern exegetical tools developed during the centuries since his *Lectures on Genesis*, (*Luther's Works* Vol. 1-8) I found that Martin Luther better understood—and had more interesting things to say about—the first book of Holy Scripture than anybody in my lifetime. It struck me that a major difference between Luther and more recent exegetes was that Luther had never heard of Julius Wellhausen!

The Documentary Hypothesis placed a kind of grid between the Text and the reader, so that the biblical materials were separated and confined into compartments that were certainly arbitrary and very likely fictitious. As a result, the story line became disjointed; literary themes and theological motifs were lost. The Text had less continuity and coherence, because the grid served as a filter, which discouraged the reader from observing its otherwise obvious features. Reading the Pentateuch became a literary variation of Ezekiel's dry and disjointed bones.

Indeed, if the reader began with the opening pages of Genesis—often regarded as a reasonable place to start the Bible—the problem arose right away, when he observed that there were two accounts of Creation.

There was nothing new in this discovery, of course. Jewish and Christian exegetes had commented on it centuries ago, and they even devised various—usually theological—theories to explain it. St. Augustine's treatment is a good example.

Now, according to Wellhausen's Documentary Hypothesis, the Creation account in chapter one of Genesis came from a post-exilic writer, who was preoccupied with priestly concerns. He was identified as the Priestly or P-Source. Following the same theory, the account in Genesis 2 was assigned to a southern writer—in Judah—who was earlier. Since this source normally used the Sacred Tetragrammaton when mentioning God, he was called the Jahvist, or J-Source. Then, having established that the two Creation accounts came from separate and independent sources, the biblical interpreter went on to demonstrate the differences between them.

Attention to such differences, however, provided no new or distinctive insights into the meaning of the Text. Those differences had been obvious to serious Bible readers for most of Christian history. The problem, it seemed to me, was this: the differences between the two accounts were not interpreted as differences *within a coherent literary unity*. It was as though the points of contrast between Hetty Sorrel and Dinah Morris had nothing to do with the literary intent of George Eliot. One would imagine that *Adam Bede* was pieced together by a combination of the HS-source and the DM-Source.

Nonetheless, assigning those two Creation accounts to two different sources did accomplish one thing: It discouraged the student of the Bible from observing rather obvious points of thematic continuity between them. Let me mention an example which Martin Luther (correctly, I believe) thought to be important.

In each of the two Creation narratives, God takes special counsel with himself with regard to a unique work of Creation. The two places are strikingly similar: In Genesis 1:26, God says, *ne'aseh 'adam*—"Let us make man." And in Genesis 2:18 He says, *'e'eseh lo*—"I will make for him...."

In fact, the Septuagint and Vulgate readings of Genesis 2:18 presuppose that the verb form in this verse is *identical* to that in 1:26—*ne'aseh*. The LXX reads *poihsomen* and the Vulgate says *faciamus*.

Both places, Luther observed, point to the "unique counsel" of God indicating the superiority of the human being over the rest of Creation: the human vocation to immortality. The second passage is an extension of the first, he said, demonstrating the woman's "share in immortality."

Over and over Genesis 1 tells us that God, beholding each thing He made, declared it to be *good: ki tov*. Only of man did He fail to make this declaration. When God looked at man, He detected a deficiency, as it were, and declared, *l'o tov*—"It is *not* good." Inasmuch as man was alone, something in Creation was missing: the household. This unfortunate situation needed a remedy, so man lost a rib to gain a home.

Luther commented on the first two chapters in 1535, when he began his *Lectures on Genesis*. This work, written between 1535 and 1545, was finished the year before he died. It arguably represents the most mature fruit of his theology, and certainly the best of his teaching on Marriage.

Luther's translation reading of Genesis 2:18 is unique in rendering the final expression as *"die um ihn sei"*—"who should be about him." He comments: "[T]he woman was so created that she should everywhere and always be about her husband." He contrasts this inseparability with the life of the animals, most of which are together only for the act of conception. On the other hand, says Luther, "among men the nature of marriage is different. There, the wife so binds herself to a man that she will be about him and will live together with him as one flesh."

Luther's high view of human sexuality is clear in the next paragraph of this work:

> For truly in all nature there was no activity more excellent and more admirable than procreation. After the proclamation of the name of God it is the most important activity Adam and Eve, in the state of innocence, could carry on—as free from sin in doing this as they were in praising God.

It is important to observe that Luther uses the expression "procreation," not "copulation." Like *all* Christians up until about 1930, Luther refused to close God's creative will out of human sexual intercourse. He believed that deliberate interference with the act of procreation was gravely sinful.

Luther commented thus on the sin of Onan:

> [T]he exceedingly foul deed of Onan, the basest of wretches ... is a most disgraceful sin. It is far more atrocious than incest and adultery. We call it unchastity, yes, a sodomitic sin. For Onan goes in to her; that is, he lies with her and copulates, and when it comes to the point of insemination, spills the semen, lest the woman conceive. Surely at such a time the order of nature established by God in procreation should be followed. Accordingly, it was a most disgraceful crime.... Consequently, he deserved to be killed by God. He committed an evil deed.

Luther commented on Marriage in other places besides his lectures on Genesis, most notably in his *The Estate of Marriage* in 1522, three years before his own marriage. In 1523, he wrote on the subject again, in his commentary on First Corinthians 7. In the next year, 1524, Luther wrote a letter to three nuns, in which he declared, "The Lord God has wanted three things made right again before the Last Day: the ministry of the Word, government, and marriage." In 1530, five years before starting the *Lectures on Genesis*, Luther published his *De Rebus Matrimonii*. In addition, he treated of marriage extensively in various places in the *Catechism*.

From his first treatment of Marriage in 1522 until the end of his life, the year after completing the *Lectures on Genesis*, Luther's treatment of Marriage was completely consistent. He rooted Marriage into the structure of human Creation. For him, it was the foundation of the home, and he believed the home was the place in which human Creation continued through procreation. Luther never separates human sexuality from God's creative act, and he believed it seriously wrong to do so.

In 1528, in his *Confession Concerning the Lord's Supper*, Luther followed the threefold pattern of concern he had expressed in 1534, in the letter to the three nuns. Luther elaborated:

> But the holy orders established by God are these three: the office of priest, the estate of marriage, the civil government.... For these three religious institutions or orders are found in God's Word and commandment; and whatever is contained in God's Word must be holy, for God's Word is holy and sanctifies everything connected with it and involved in it. Above these three institutions and orders is the common order of Christian love, in which one serves not only the three orders but also serves every needy person in general with all kinds of benevolent deeds, such as feeding the hungry, giving drink to

the thirsty, forgiving enemies, praying for all men on earth, suffering all kinds of evil on earth, etc. Behold these are called good and holy works.

It is nearly impossible to overestimate the place of Marriage in Luther's concept of the Reform of the Church. I quote from the historian, Lyndal Roper:

When, in 1532, Luther meditated on the central goals of the reformation of the Church, which he had set in motion, he numbered the changes in the institution of marriage as amongst the most important. Protestant reformers devoted much of their energies to condemning what they considered immorality, to promoting the estate of marriage, and to restoring what they regarded as the 'right order' in marriage and the household. Their articulation of a morality of sexuality and marriage had profound implications for Protestants' understanding of what it is to he a man or woman. By examining Lutheran views of illicit sex, marriage and the household, we can begin to unravel the connections between the Protestants' conceptions of masculinity and femininity on the one hand, and their advocacy of the proper order in marriage and household on the other.

Let me close with a quotation of Luther, from a wedding sermon given in 1531. By this time, he had been married for six years and had experienced the joys of a wife and children. He said:

God's Word is actually inscribed on one's spouse. When a man looks at his wife as if she were the only woman on earth, and when a woman looks at her husband as if he were the only man on earth; yes, if no king or queen, not even the sun itself sparkles any more brightly and lights up your eyes more than your own husband or wife, then right there you are face to face with God speaking. God promises to you your wife or husband, actually gives your spouse to you saying, "The man shall be yours. I am pleased beyond measure! Creatures earthly and heavenly are jumping for joy." For there is no jewelry more precious than God's Word; through it you come to regard your spouse as a gift of God and, as long as you do that, you have no regrets."

Patrick Henry Reardon is the pastor of All Saints Orthodox Church in Chicago and a Senior Editor of *Touchstone: A Journal of Mere Christianity*. Educated many years ago at Southern Baptist Theological Seminary in Louisville and the Pontificio Instituto Biblico in Rome, Father Reardon is the author of *Christ in the Psalms, Christ in His Saints, The Trial of Job, Chronicles of History and Worship, Genesis: Creation and the Patriarchal Histories*, and, most recently, *Wise Lives*, a commentary on the Book of Sirach.

Pygmalion Redeemed: The Christ-Centered Imperative of Marriage

Nathan Yoder

Pygmalion

It is centuries before the invention of the clock,
And there is no window in that musty stonecutter's shop—
But knowing artists, it's certain to be early in the morning dark:
Pygmalion's candles are burned to messy stubs,
Aurora lurks about the city, a vacant smile in her eye, and
Apollo thunders across that last stretch of sky before Athens.

He was admiring his handiwork, running a hand down
the small of her cold, white back,
Tracing smooth curves he'd wrought
with such precision mere moments before,
When she turned around and winked at him—
Suddenly, it was he who was made of stone.

His hammer lies where it fell to the floor.
And now she bends to him, and now a sigh, a smile, a kiss.
She is now fluid as milk, and he is transfixed:
Taut, angular, muscles in bewildered arms that hold,
Impossibly, her—

That blushing in his cheek betrays the storytellers:
It was she who gave life to him.

—Joshua Howard Yoder
May, 2003

So penned my brother, doubtless in the dark before dawn; a bachelor inspired by muse as yet unknown. He married her some years later. Addressing the couple and assembled guests, my father recited this poem from Joshua's undergraduate days and addressed its proleptic import. Joshua had written it in *anticipation* of Jennifer. Like the sculptor in question, the poet had also desired a companion, one to complement him and enhance, to challenge and confound. Not a bride of his design, but a blessing of providence. Such is the true moral of the myth: not that man chiseled a goddess out of marble, but that heaven graced him with the love of his life.

God alone can bestow such a boon as married love. So argued Luther in 1519. Katie yet unknown and the possibility of marriage never fathomed, a celibate Augustinian offered an exegesis of Genesis 2 that reads for all the world as if it were composed by a husband and lover of one woman over the span of decades.

> If God himself does not give the wife or the husband, anything can happen... Adam found no marriageable partner for himself, but as soon as God had created Eve and *brought her to him, he felt a real married love toward her, and recognized that she was his wife.* Those who want to enter into the estate of marriage should learn from this that they should earnestly pray to God for a spouse.[1]

So it was with Adam: in constant communication with his creation, God perceived the man's loneliness and made provision, plain and simple. "He brings her to him, he gives her to him; and Adam agrees to accept her. Therefore, that is what marriage is."[2] A pious request and the willingness to have it granted in the course of time: these are the only prerequisites necessary to participate in what was meant to become "the greatest and purest of all loves ... a bride's love, which glows like a fire and desires nothing but the husband.

---

1. *Luther's Works*, American Edition, 55 vols., eds. J. Pelikan and H. Lehmann (St. Louis & Philadelphia: Concordia & Fortress, 1955ff.) 44:8 [hereafter cited as LW].
2. LW 44, 8.

She says, 'It is you I want, not what is yours: I want neither your silver nor your gold; I want neither. I want only you. I want you in your entirety, or not at all."[3] This holistic longing conveys *eros* in its ideal: a totality of body and soul, a dedication to a fuller quality of life in which true intercourse involves the complete dedication of the self for the other.

The Lutheran tradition continues this invocation of the nobility of *eros*. Adolf von Harless calls marriage the highest, most complete form of human community this side of the Kingdom.[4] At its purest, *eros* is kenotic and sacrificial: longing for the other entails the emptying of self. In marriage it finds its soil, and from its vines sprout all other human relationships. Paul Althaus likewise calls marriage and family the *arche* of community, "an indispensable condition of life [that] provides in its own right the means for wholeness."[5] But all is contingent upon the mutual acceptance of the blessing. Considering Luther's admonition that one accept and cherish the gift of the spouse, it is ironic that he failed to give the groom, the husband, an answering voice. One imagines it would go something like this: "You have me, all that I am, and I give my all; as *husband*, as cultivator, I will give all that I am that you and our children should reach your full potential." Pure *eros* cherishes the uniqueness of the bride. Whether the medieval model of arranged marriage that looks for love to grow from the promise, or the post-Romantic view that fastens the promise where love has already taken root: it is the uniqueness and the totality of the other as wife, as husband, that is cherished and celebrated. So said the theologian; and so it was with stonecutter and statue.

---

3. LW 44, 9.

4. Gottlieb Christoph Adolf von Harless, *Die Christliche Ethik*. 8th and partially extended edition (Gütersloh: C. Bertelsmann, 1893), 522.

5. Paul Althaus, *Theologie der Ordnungen* (Gütersloh: C. Bertelsmann, 1935), 9.

If "Pygmalion" adequately conveys *eros* in its purity, another myth masterfully captures its distortion:

Look not in my eyes, for fear
They mirror true the sight I see,
And there you find your face too clear
And love it and be lost like me.
One the long nights through must lie
Spent in star-defeated sighs,
But why should you as well as I
Perish? gaze not in my eyes.

A Grecian lad, as I hear tell,
One that many loved in vain,
looked into a forest well
and never looked away again.
There, when the turf in springtime flowers,
With downward eye and gazes sad,
Stands amid the glancing showers
A jonquil, not a Grecian lad.

—A. E. Housman

The descent of Narcissus into watery oblivion shows well the formless void that sexuality can become under the fall. As his name suggests—*narcosis*—he became increasingly numb to the lack of substance in the visage that met his gaze. Content with the superficial, he reveled in ripples and shadows. Pygmalion knew his medium was stone, not flesh; hence his appeal to the gods. Narcissus made no such appeal, perfectly happy to stare at a puddle until he starved to death—or perhaps, in fitting irony, died of thirst; the myth doesn't spell it out. Just so, the consequences of sexual chaos are starvation and thirst: starved for substance, parched for lack of life. It is not the other in her entirety that is desired: it is rather the function she can provide. It is not the beauty of her person but the *prosopon*, the mask of beauty without life, without story. This numbness characterizes what Helmut Thielicke termed the "breakdown of personal being," the debasement of the self through the sexual degradation of others.[6] "There is something like a communism in the erotic," continues Thielicke. "It evidences itself in the fact that that which evokes the peripheral manifestations of eroticism are present everywhere as public property in the form of sex appeal."[7] This ubiquity of pornography is what Luther calls the "false love" of *curvatus in se*, the fallacy that believes that the self can be elevated at the expense of the other's humanity. False *eros*, wrote Luther, does not long for the other. "It seeks its own: money, honor, possessions, women taken outside of marriage and against God's command."[8] Dying of thirst while drowning in our own passions: such is the truth of Narcissus: that *eros* bears the indelible blot of the Fall. "Cursed is the ground because of you" (Gen 3:17). Humankind turned inward upon itself and perished. And the very flowers wept.

Marriage as Corrective

The narcosis of Adam and Eve makes the notion of ideal *eros* a myth—even in marriage. False love and true are rolled together. Luther is quick to offer this qualification of the "greatest and purest of all loves."[9] The covenant is not what it would have been: under sin, it becomes a preventive medicine, "a hospital for incurables which prevents inmates from falling into graver

---

6. Helmut Thielicke, *The Ethics of Sex*, trans. John W. Doberstein (New York: Harper and Row, 1964), 24.

7. Thielicke, 25.

8. LW 44, 9.

9. LW 44, 8.

sin."[10] Chastity apart from marriage, in thought and deed, is "hardly possible, and without special grace from God, quite impossible."[11] Marriage, the union of one woman and one man, counters the carnal points of *curvatus in se* and makes an obligation out of an otherwise mortal sin. But though fidelity restricts the scope of lust, it cannot extinguish it. And so marriage becomes a vehicle for the *lex semper accusat*, the ever-accusing Law of God.

In the Fall, Pygmalion devolves into Narcissus. The warmth and fluidity of the miracle become, in sin, as stone once more, superficial gratification that ignores the beauty of the bride's very being. He sees only himself in her eyes, and is lost. The same curse extends to the children; they too become as objects. "False natural love," chides Luther, "blinds parents so that they have more regard for the bodies of their children than they have for their souls."[12] Harless called this sort of affection *Affenliebe*, ape-like love that seeks ultimate fulfillment in offspring rather than in service to the God who granted them.[13]

Marriage and family as order of creation thus stand under law. They may restrict the landscape of sin to a given locality, but not the degree of its severity within their boundaries. Luther puts it simply: "Nowhere [in Scripture] do we read that the man who marries a wife receives any grace of God."[14] The camel could traverse the needle's eye before Pygmalion could avoid the inevitable narcosis of tainted love.

---

10. LW 44, 9.

11. LW 44, 9.

12. LW 44, 13.

13. Harless, 545.

14. LW 36, 92.

Marriage, Family, and Incarnation

> "Who then can be saved?" But Jesus looked at them and said, "With man this is impossible, but with God all things are possible" (Matt 19:25-26).

Part of the answer to *cur deus homo* can be answered simply as, "to set love aright." If Luther is right, and the ideal *eros* of Eden was the noblest and purest form of love under the sun—a complete dedication of the self to the other, from which spring forth all human relationships—then the cure for its corruption requires the advent of a divine love to cement itself within the webs of *eros* and *storge*, and so redeem them. In accordance with the will of God, this advent occurred in response to an acceptance of a gift, twice over. Luke gives the steadfast bride her voice: "Let it be according to your word." Matthew simply records the bridegroom's tacit obedience. But the bottom line is that the One in whom all things were made became a human being in the dark of a virgin's womb, and was born into a family: nurtured by natural love, but ever about His Father's business. In Christ Jesus, *agape* confronts and dispels the sinful finality that *eros* and *storge* have assumed for themselves. *Who is my mother, and who are my brothers?* (Matt 12:48). And yet, divine love does not abandon human love, even when *agape* itself was forsaken by its very source. *Woman, behold your son* (Jn 19:26).

The Sacramental Question

In his 1519 *Sermon on the Estate of Marriage*, Luther goes so far as to name marriage a sacrament. The following year in *On the Babylonian Captivity*, he declares quite the opposite: that marriage as creation under the Fall conveys no redemptive significance. But his initial claim was made on the grounds that the union of woman and man is an *anticipation* and *indication* of the union of the divine and the human in Christ Jesus.

It is indeed a wonderful sacrament that the estate of marriage truly signifies such a great reality. Is it not a wonderful thing that God is man and that he gives himself to man and will be his, just as the husband gives himself to his wife and is hers? But if God is ours, then everything is ours.[15]

The fullness of the marriage bond thus anticipates the fulfillment of all creation in the Risen Lord. For marriages under the cross, however, this anticipation is not mere metaphor. They participate in the Paschal Mystery.

He that does not love does not love God, for God is love (1 Jn 4:8).

God is love; and for the sake of the world, all the majesty of God has become human in Jesus of Nazareth. Therefore, *agape* does not and cannot exist apart from the Incarnation of Jesus Christ. In pitching the tent among us, the love of God entered fully into human relationships, beginning with family. In this encounter of the event of Jesus Christ we beheld the glory of God, as of a Father's Only Son, full of grace and truth (Jn 1:14). And in the concrete encounters of human existence we behold His eternal love at work in human agency; in *Theotokoi*, bearers of God in the power of the Holy Spirit. This love is present both in moments of acute distress, such as the tragically ubiquitous scenario played out on the road to Jericho, and in the banalities of the routine.

We who are in Christ have to recognize perpetually that every moment of every relationship, every human encounter, however brief, is governed by our ontology as *Kaine Ktisis*, new creation in the death and resurrection of our Lord. As marriage and family are

---

15. LW 44, 10. Cf. LW 31, *A Sermon on Two Kinds of Righteousness*, 300. "Therefore through the first righteousness arises the voice of the bridegroom who says to the soul, 'I am yours,' but through the second comes the voice of the bride who answers, 'I am yours.' Then the marriage is consummated; it becomes strong and complete."

the seminal relationships from which spring all subsequent human contact, how vital it is that we should see the Word of God, redeemed *imago dei*, in spouse and child! If one cannot see his bride as a child of God, how can he look with *agape* on the bloody bigot bleeding in the ditch? How can he love his enemy?

Joined to Christ, and grasping that vocation to cling to his bond, in faith, one finds the haze of fallen *eros* lifting. Pygmalion had become Narcissus, petrified in demonic parody of his bride's quickening. His eyes darkened and he could not see the gift of marriage for what it was intended to be. The glowing fire of *eros* had flared and died, a spot of flame to dry grass that consumed the other and then was gone.

But in the face of this hellish, nihilistic fate, we join Luther in this declaration: "But I am baptized! And if I am baptized, I have the promise that I shall be saved and have eternal life, both in soul and body."[16] In Christ and in Him alone, the husband can see the bride, the mother can see the child, without the false mirror of Narcissus and his malaise between them. In living water and the Word, the Holy Spirit penetrates the looking glass. They see darkly, qualifies St. Paul; certainly not as they will see at the marriage feast to come. But even so: reality shines through, more and more as life in the Spirit waxes. It is therefore in their *baptism*, in their belonging to Christ and their acceptance of this destiny in faith, that husband and wife can take account of each other beyond the veneer of erotic utility. For where *eros* conveys subjective worth, *agape* brings realization of authentic being. Helmut Thielicke argues it so: "*Agape* realizes itself in this realm by permeating the given—and necessarily given—*eros* relationship."[17] To employ Martin Chemnitz's Christological language, there is a "true and real" permeating of human love with divine love in the Holy Spirit, a *communicatio*

---

16. Martin Luther, *Large Catechism, in The Book of Concord*, trans. and ed. Theodore G. Tappert (Philadelphia: Fortress Press, 1959), 442.

17. Thielicke, 103.

idiomatum as iron is infused with fire in the forge.[18] The alien righteousness that comes to woman and man in the real presence of Christ Jesus in the Eucharist joins in, with, and under *eros* in marriage. God provides the fire, and Luther's invocation of the bride's love is validated. The desired one, unique in all the ranks of humanity, is also one "who has been bought with a price" (1 Cor 6:20; 7:23). In the words of Thielicke, this creature "has a temporal and eternal destiny, a destiny in which one who claims this other person in his totality responsibly participates."[19] Marriage thus not only signifies the union of Christ with his church—it *partakes* of it. My wife is no longer simply bone of *my* bone, flesh of *my* flesh. As a member of the body of Christ, she possesses an alien dignity bestowed upon her by the Most High, and her love in Christ Jesus for me is a visible Word, an embodied execution of the Gospel. The Confessions leave the question of the number of sacraments open for just this rationale. As with penance, marriage could easily be classified—and certainly should be!—within the umbrella of baptism. But its essential quality of union, *community*, gives it a unique phenotype within the spectrum of baptismal existence. Thielicke nails it down: "The order of creation and the order of redemption converge in the symbol of marriage."[20] Harless agrees:

> The divinely-ordered natural basis of the entire earthly-human corporate being is the ethical personal community of marriage and the family which springs from it, whose communal bond is personal piety and love: mutual giving and taking, leading and allowing oneself to be led. In the name of spouse, father, brother, and sister, this bond carries the natural prototype of that highest form of community, the [binding of] human beings to-

---

18. Eric W. Gritsch and Robert W. Jenson, *Lutheranism. The Theological Movement and Its Confessional Writings* (Philadelphia: Fortress Press, 1976), 99.

19. Thielicke, 25.

20. Thielicke, 108.

gether in Christ and each other in holy and transfigured fulfillment.[21]

There is a twofold Christ-centered rubric that categorizes this holy estate. The community of husband and wife is a creature, brought into being through the *Logos*. In light of Easter morning, the two, each *Kaine Ktisis*, embody the love of God for each other—and all others—as they travel the way, companions in the One who was revealed to them in the breaking of the bread. And the *Paraclete* is there, bringing forth faith within the marriage covenant to hold fast to grace and accomplish the redemptive, strange work of God.

The Vocational Imperative

Recognizing that marriage is an object rather than a source of divine love, and that husband and wife are recipients of the alien righteousness of Jesus Christ, the question now becomes: what sort of *proper* righteousness will the love of God affect in them? What unique fruit will their love, *eros* and *agape*, produce? One that reflects that dual Christocentrism. Created in God's image, the two are called to be a vehicle for God to bring forth new human beings. Redeemed by the blood of the Savior, the two share in the New Commandment and the Great Commission. Therefore, in Christ, the life of faith of the married couple has the holistic *telos* of the home: conceiving, bearing, and rearing disciples of Jesus Christ, in the church. For Luther, this is where faith is best exemplified.

> But this at least all married people should know. They can do no better work and do nothing more valuable either for God, for Christendom, for all the world, for themselves and for their children than to bring up their

---

21. Harless, 518. Cf. LW, 44, 10. "In the same way the estate of marriage is a sacrament. It is an outward and spiritual sign of the greatest, holiest, worthiest, and noblest thing that has ever existed or ever will exist: the union of the divine and human natures of Christ."

children well. In comparison with this one work, that married people should bring up their children properly, there is nothing at all in pilgrimages to Rome, Jerusalem... nothing at all in building churches, endowing masses, or whatever good works could be named. For bringing up their children properly is their shortest road to heaven. In fact, heaven itself could not be made nearer or achieved more easily than by doing this work. It is also their appointed work. Where parents are not conscientious about this, it is as if everything were the wrong way around, like fire that will not burn or water that is not wet.[22]

Marriage is therefore the complete union under God of all baptismal vocation and destiny between the sexes, and the sharing of a new vocation that qualifies all the others: to conceive, bear, and love children for the glory of God.

These are categorical commands. Pygmalion sculpts anew; from the bodies of wife and husband, from the hands that labor and the longing that achieves being, God gives a new gift. In family, *agape* does for *storge* what it did for *eros*. Whether a pulse of being in the warm dark of the womb or a child come of age, mother and father see their child through the cross, through the empty tomb, and know that *this* one is marked for the eternal service of the Lord. Authentic, eschatological being qualifies subjective worth.[23] My child, kicking-baby-in-the-belly or tantrum-teen-pain-in-the-rear, is first and foremost God's child in Jesus Christ, given me at God's discretion, not mine. There is no other model for the family of faith. Biology may work against us; infirmity may make conception impossible. That is the reality of the Fall. But the imperative of parenthood

22. LW 44, 12.

23. Cf. Thielicke, 28: "In *eros* the *worth* of the other person is the object; in *agape* the *authentic being* [*Eigentlichkeit*] of the other person is the object."

remains, the *telos* of the home endures, and there are myriads of children longing for the union of natural and divine love that the Christian family is called to provide.

A Memory of Baptism

It was in the morning dark that Brayden came into the world. Technology had failed me in the form of a faulty cell tower, and so the message arrived in the age-old way: a knock at the door. An anxious grandfather stood there and said, "it's time." The baby, the second pregnancy for the young couple, was gravely damaged; part of his organs had grown outside of his body, and there was no hope of prolonged survival outside of the womb. In prior discussions with his parents, they had voiced an unprompted declaration that they were called to nurture him as long as God allowed. They did so without question, without hesitance, immersed—there is no other way to put it—in a peace beyond my understanding. Brayden was born before dawn, and I baptized him in the name of the Father, and of the Son, and of the Holy Spirit. And ten minutes later, with mother and father holding him and me, we commended him to God. A lamb of Christ's own flock, a sinner of his own redeeming. An event for doctor, nurse, family and pastor to ponder in their hearts for the rest of their lives.

This work of the Holy Spirit—the alien righteousness of water and the Word, and the proper righteousness of the parents that bore Brayden to that place, that day—was possible only in the One who grew in Mary's womb in answer to her obedience, who entered humanity through the Holy Family. Her blood gave Him life; the hands of the carpenter formed Him in stature. But in the culmination of all history, all community, in the dark before dawn, God disproved the myths and the wisdom of the world. For it was Christ who gave life to *Mary*.

A Final Admonition

Members of the Body of Christ with plans of marriage in their hearts, and those charged with the care of their souls, need to take a good, hard look at the two pericopes used so often in weddings that they have become as clichés. For love is of God, and everyone who loves is born of God and knows God (1 Jn 4:7). And love bears all things, believes all things, hopes all things, endures all things (1 Cor 13:7). Bride and groom need to understand the Incarnation of God in Jesus Christ and what it means for them and their family. The need to understand the foundation of *agape* underlying and transforming their love for each other, and for their children, calling them to die to the old Adam, the old narcosis. They need to know that God is joining—categorically, utterly—their vocations and destinies completely into the home, indelibly forging Matthew 28 to Genesis 1:28. They need to know that their specific, unique marriage, which bears the underlying essential essence of an order of creation, is also a sign in anticipation of the eternal marriage feast to come. And they need to know that they are to exemplify the life in Christ for each other and their children: a love for them and for the world that glows with the fire of the Gospel:

> You have me, all that I am, and I give my all; I will give all that I am that you and your children should reach your full potential in me. It is you I want, not what is yours: I want neither your silver nor your gold; I want neither. I want only you. I want you in your entirety, or not at all.

The Rev. Nathan H. Yoder, STS, is Pastor at St. Martin's Lutheran Church in Maiden, NC. He successfully defended his doctoral dissertation in Systematic Theology at the University of Regensburg, Germany, in July 2011. He is a member of the Society of the Holy Trinity and a pastor in the North American Lutheran Church, Carolinas Chapter.

Taking Refuge with Luther

Brad Everett

There is a legend concerning a prophet sent by God to speak His word to the inhabitants of a sinful city. The prophet did as God directed and soon was found walking the city streets, proclaiming the Word of the LORD in the hope the people would hear and repent. However, this was a particularly wicked city and his message fell on deaf ears and hard hearts—so much so that to his knowledge none had repented. Being a faithful and obedient prophet, he continued doing as God had instructed, regardless of the results. Sometime later he was found standing at a street corner, shouting the Word he had been given at the top of his lungs. He looked quite mad and so a passerby stopped and asked the prophet, "You do realize that no one is listening? Nothing you say is going to change these people or this city." The prophet replied, "When I began preaching I did so with the hope of changing this city. Now I am preaching the Word of the LORD with the hope that this city doesn't change me."

The mandate of the Lake Louise Commission plainly states the condition of the society we find ourselves in—how beliefs and practices concerning marriage and family that were not accepted by society less than 100 years ago, are today seen as ordinary—so much so that in some cases segments of the Church have pronounced God's blessing on them.

One approach to this situation might be to mount an offensive, marshalling a wide-range of arguments from Scripture and Tradition to confront these lies in an effort to bring change. While there is much to commend such an approach, some, myself included, are weary of this fighting and struggle. We find ourselves so "sick and tired of being mad as hell," at what is going on in society, (and for some of us, what's going on in our denominations), that we fear protracted polemics will leave us bitter and jaded, neither of which is becoming for followers of Christ. Like the prophet of legend, we know we need to continue to faithfully declare the message given to us by God, but also like the prophet, we do so less to try and convert the world around us (which is the work of the Spirit and not us anyway) but to keep ourselves from being changed, from even entertaining the question "Did God really say...?"

Ironically it is to one of the Church's renowned polemicists that we can turn for support and relief in the midst of this distress. The writings of Martin Luther concerning marriage and family life are a gift to the Church. Firmly grounded in Scripture and also Tradition (of course insofar as it did not contradict Scripture), he holds up for all to see, God's graciousness in creating these institutions and the blessedness of man and woman to be able to participate in them. What Luther wrote on these matters was not terribly original, but it was the way he wrote. Luther's concern was not just to write and preach for the scholars and pastors of his day, but also for the average Hans and Greta that they might be encouraged in their faith, and grow in their love, knowledge and service of Christ. Such a clear presentation of God's intention for marriage and family based on Scripture is truly a blessing in this day and age when we are given everything but. The challenges and pitfalls Luther addresses aren't so different from those facing us today, and of course the blessings and promises of God never change.

Even though he initially had no intention of marrying himself, Luther had a high view of marriage as evidenced in his 1522 treatise "Estate of Marriage." Luther wrote of marriage in glowing terms, but to cut off possible detractors said:

> I will not mention the other advantages and delights implicit in a marriage that goes well—that husband and wife cherish one another, become one, serve one another, and other attendant blessings—lest someone shut me up by saying I am speaking about something I have not experienced, and there is more gall than honey in marriage. I base my remarks on Scripture, which to me is surer than all experience and cannot lie to me.[1]

Note Luther's confidence in Scripture as the Word of God, and its predominance over his or anyone's experience. This is an emphasis found throughout his work, to place one's trust and hope in nothing else or less than the Word of God, no matter if one is discussing the forgiveness of sins and feelings of guilt, or the challenges of marriage and family.

Luther's confidence in the witness of Scripture was well placed as he finally married Katherine von Bora in 1525, one of 12 nuns he helped smuggle from a convent two years earlier. She was the last to find a husband and it was only at the encouragement of colleagues that he even considered taking her as his wife. There was no sense of romance on Luther's part, who gave as his three reasons for his marriage "to please his father, to spite the pope and the Devil, and to seal his witness before martyrdom."[2] While he suspected martyrdom would mean being burned at the stake, his witness instead was through 20 years of marriage to his beloved Katie with whom he raised a family of six children. Some of Luther's comments on marriage and family are well known, such as after years of being a bachelor the shock of waking in the morning and

---

1. Martin Luther, "Estate of Marriage" *Luther's Works Vol. 45 The Christian in Society* (Philadelphia: Muhlenberg Press, 1962), 43.

2. Roland H. Bainton, *Here I Stand* (Nashville: Abingdon, 1950), 288.

seeing pigtails on the pillow next to him or referring to Katie as "my lord." However, for many, anecdotes are as far as they have plumbed the depths of Luther's writing on the gifts of marriage and family. Skipping along the surface of his witticisms, they have missed the intensity of Luther's writings on what for him was a crucial subject. In his Confessional writings as well as his other works, Luther consistently holds up the blessedness of spouse and children. In a day when marriage and family are being denigrated or at the very least diminished from seemingly every quarter, it is encouraging to hear from one who holds them in high regard, and gives others every reason to do the same.

When making reference to Luther and his writings on any subject it is crucial to differentiate between his contribution to works that make up the Lutheran Confessions contained in *The Book of Concord* and the rest of his writings. For Lutherans, the Confessions are considered to be faithful expositions of Scripture and thus carry a degree of authority derived from Scripture. However, Luther's other works carry no such authority, and Luther had no delusions about this. When asked by printers in Augsburg and Wittenberg for permission to publish his collected works he said:

> I'd rather that all my books would disappear and the Holy Scriptures alone be read. Otherwise we'll rely on such writings and let the Bible go... Who wants to buy such stout tomes? And if they're bought who will read them? And if they're read who'll be edified by them?[3]

The attention given to marriage in the Lutheran Confessions typically centers on the issue of clerical celibacy—the exception being Luther's discussion of the matter in his Small and Large Catechisms, in particular in his handling of the Fourth and Sixth Commandments.

---

3. Martin Luther, "Proposal to Publish Luther's Collected Works" *Luther's Works Vol. 54 Table Talk* (Philadelphia: Fortress Press, 1967), 311.

The Fourth Commandment "You are to honor your father and mother" contains an underlying assertion of the importance of the marriage relationship between husband and wife who, properly speaking, are also father and mother.

> God has given this walk of life, fatherhood and motherhood, a special position of honor, higher than that of any other walk of life under it. Not only has he commanded us to love parents but to honor them. ...[H]e distinguishes father and mother above all other persons on earth, and places them next to himself.[4]

While the heathens may do otherwise, for Christians it is within the marriage relationship that children are conceived, nourished and nurtured. As co-creators with God, parents bear a particular responsibility to God, their children and by extension to the church and society in how they carry out the parental vocation. Luther writes:

> They [parents] should keep in mind that they owe obedience to God, and that, above all they should earnestly and faithfully discharge the duties of their office not only to provide material support for their children...but especially to bring them up to the praise and honor of God. Therefore do not imagine that the parental office is a matter of your pleasure and whim. It is a strict commandment of and injunction of God, who holds you accountable for it.[5]

Luther goes on to stress the magnitude of this commandment noting that children are not given for our pleasure or amusement, but that they have been entrusted to the care of their parents

---

4. Martin Luther, "Large Catechism" *The Book of Concord: The Confessions of the Evangelical Lutheran Church*, eds. Robert Kolb and Timothy J. Wengert (Minneapolis: Fortress Press, 2000), 400-401.

5. Ibid., 409.

who are to spare no effort, time or expense in teaching the children to serve God and the world. Luther clearly sets out parental priorities, warning against thinking only of gaining money and property for the children (as if God were unable or unwilling to provide for them). Rather, he emphasizes that it is the parents' chief duty "first to bring up their children in the fear and knowledge of God, and, then, if they are so gifted, also to have them engage in formal study and learn so they may be of service wherever they are needed."[6] The honor that the fourth commandment rules is due parents, is because of the duties and responsibilities God has placed on them to raise up faithful children into faithful adults so that His relationship with His people might continue.

Luther next addresses the issues of marriage and family in the Sixth Commandment, "You are not to commit adultery." He notes that while the Fourth Commandment endorsed the marriage relationship, the Sixth serves to protect it because God wishes us to:

> [H]onor, maintain and cherish it as a divine and blessed walk of life. He has established it before all others as the first of all institutions, and he created man and woman differently (as is evident) not for indecency but to be true to each other, to be fruitful, to beget children, and to nurture and bring them up to the glory of God....Married life is no matter for jest or idle curiosity, but it is a glorious institution and an object of God's serious concern.[7]

This also reflects Augustine's understanding of the three goods of marriage: procreation or fruitfulness, chastity or faithfulness and bonding or fellowship.[8]

---

6. Ibid., 410.

7. Ibid., 414.

8. *Proles, fides, et sacramentum.* Douglas Farrow, *Nation of Bastards* (Toronto: BPS Books, 207), 16.

In language that sounds strange to 21st Century ears, Luther describes marriage not just as an honorable walk of life, but a necessary one, solemnly commanded by God in general for both men and women from all walks of life as the reason for which they were created. He notes that to be sure there are some rare exceptions whom God has exempted—those unsuited to married life or those whom God has given the gift of maintaining chastity outside of marriage.[9] Because it is God who has exempted these individuals they are to be encouraged knowing that their circumstance, if not the norm, is still part of God's intention for them.

In his concluding words on the Sixth Commandment, Luther emphasizes the importance of husband and wife cherishing the spouse given to them, living in love and harmony in perfect fidelity, so that chastity may follow without any command—which is why, he says, St. Paul admonishes couples to love and honor each other (Eph. 5:22, 25; Col. 3:18-19).[10]

To bring this into even sharper focus, consider what Luther says in his explanation of the First Commandment "You are to have no other gods," earlier in the Large Catechism. Contrasting those who have placed their faith in the true God with those whose faith is in something else (e.g. wealth, learning, power, honor etc.) he stresses that what is presented in this commandment (and by extension those that follow) is the very Word and promise of God. "Therefore let everyone take this to heart and thus be careful not to regard this as if a mere human being were speaking. ...Unfortunately, the world neither believes this nor regards it as God's Word."[11]

Thus, these commandments and the rest of Scripture are not merely human constructs for us to debate, reject or accept on the basis of our own standards or understanding. Rather they are given

---

9. Ibid., 414-415.
10. Ibid., 415-416.
11. Ibid., 391.

that we may know God's gracious will for us, so we can live the lives to which we have been called in our baptism. As the Word of God, here we find all good and refuge in all need.[12] So too can we find refuge and encouragement in Luther's writings, which are grounded in God's Word.

In his commentaries on Scripture, Luther unfailingly writes of the blessedness of marriage as ordained and instituted by God. Even when discussing divorce he finds a way to hold up God's intention for men and women in marriage.

> ...[I]t would be a real art and a very strong safeguard against all this [divorce, lust, unchastity] if everyone learned to look at his spouse correctly according to God's Word, which is the dearest treasure and loveliest ornament you can find in a man or a woman. ...Though I look over all the women in the world, I cannot find any about whom I can boast with a joyful conscience as I can about mine: 'This is the one whom God has granted to me and put into my arms.' I know that He and all the angels are heartily pleased if I cling to her lovingly and faithfully. Then why should I despise this precious gift of God and take up with someone else, where I can find no such treasure or adornment?[13]

With regards to children, parenthood was an expected consequence and the greatest blessing of marriage.

> But the greatest good in married life, that which makes all suffering and labor worth while, is that God grants offspring and commands that they be brought up to worship and serve him. In all the world this is the noblest

---

12. Ibid., 386.

13. Martin Luther, "The Sermon on the Mount" *Luther's Works Vol. 21 The Sermon on the Mount and The Magnificat* (St. Louis: Concordia Publishing House, 1956), 87.

and most precious work, because there is nothing dearer than the salvation of souls.[14]

While the salvation of souls is dear to God, that didn't preclude Divine interest in the other aspects of parental duties in raising children.

> Now you tell me, when a father goes ahead and washes diapers or performs some other mean task for his child, and someone ridicules him as an effeminate fool—though that father is acting in the spirit just described and in Christian faith—my dear fellow you tell me, which of the two is most keenly ridiculing the other? God, with all his angels and creatures is smiling—not because that father is washing diapers, but because he is doing so in Christian faith. Those who sneer at him and see only the task and not the faith are ridiculing God with all his creatures, as the biggest fool on earth. Indeed, they are only ridiculing themselves; with all their cleverness they are nothing but the devil's fools.[15]

Clearly, Luther understood that every aspect in the care and raising of children was blessed by God as part of the parental vocation. Children were a gift of God and were to be treated with the respect and love due them as such.

The contraceptive mentality we have today would have been foreign to Luther (as it was to any Christian prior to the 1930s when various Protestant denominations began permitting it). Parenthood was not something to be delayed, denied or managed (i.e. "how many children do you want?"), but was a gift bestowed by God to be graciously received.

---

14. Martin Luther, "Estate of Marriage" *Luther's Works Vol. 45 The Christian in Society* (Philadelphia: Muhlenberg Press, 1962), 46.

15. Ibid., 40.

To see how Luther viewed one who engaged in intercourse and tried to prevent pregnancy consider his commentary on Genesis 38:9-10 and the case of Onan.

> Onan must have been a malicious and incorrigible scoundrel. This is a most disgraceful sin. It is far more atrocious than incest and adultery. We call it unchastity, yes, a Sodomitic sin. For Onan goes into her; that is he lies with her and copulates, and when it comes time to the point of insemination, spills the semen, lest the woman conceive. Surely at such a time the order of nature established by God in procreation should be followed.... Consequently, he deserved to be killed by God. He committed an evil deed. Therefore God punished him.[16]

Strong words to be sure, but fitting when considered in the context of the rest of Luther's writing on marriage and family. It could be argued that Onan's main sin was that he abdicated his duty to continue his dead brother's lineage (serious enough to be sure). But the significance of the form that his avoidance took cannot be ignored. Family and children are considered a blessing from God, and Onan deprived his brother's family of that blessing. Not just by refusing to sleep with his sister-in-law, but by engaging with her in the procreative act and then pre-empting conception.

As one might expect, even the common objection of not being able to adequately support oneself let alone a family, Luther says shows nothing less than a lack of faith and doubt of God's goodness and truth.[17] If one hasn't been exempted from the vocation of marriage and in fact has been gifted with a spouse, then one

---

16. Martin Luther, *Luther's Works Vol. 7 Lectures on Genesis Chapters 38-44* (Saint Louis: Concordia Publishing House, 1965), 21.

17. Ibid., 47.

should trust that God will generously support this family as taught in the Fourth Petition of the Lord's Prayer, "Give us today our daily bread."[18]

Living in this fallen and sinful world, sometimes pregnancy and childbirth ended in miscarriage or stillbirth. For parents, and especially mothers, facing such grief, Luther wrote a brief piece entitled "Comfort For Women Who Have Had A Miscarriage."[19] In it he consoles them that they need not fear God is angry with them or that in death their children have been abandoned by God, but offers assurance of God's care for both the parents and the child. This is of a piece with Luther's understanding that parenthood is a vocation to which God has called mothers and fathers, so it is to be expected that God's care and support would also include tragic circumstances like these.

One could continue to mine Luther's works for additional treasures on marriage and family and have their efforts greatly rewarded. Through exegesis of Scripture Luther outlined God's gracious intention for men and women to become husbands and wives, and eventually fathers and mothers. In his own marriage and family, Luther bore witness that his experience was as blessed as God's Word promised. So where does that leave us today?

As mentioned at the outset, polemics and apologetics around the issues of marriage and family are important and necessary— but not at the risk of harming our own spiritual health and that of our families. It would be foolishness to squander or miss out on the blessings of the gift of family while fighting for it on whatever front. Instead let's take Luther's writings on marriage and family as a refuge and an encouragement in these troubled times—first for ourselves, and then take what we have gained and share it with

18. See Luther's Small Catechism, 357, and Large Catechism 449-452.

19. Martin Luther, "Comfort For Women Who Have Had A Miscarriage" *Luther's Works Vol. 43 Devotional Writings II* (Philadelphia: Fortress Press, 1968), 247-250.

those around us. Like the prophet mentioned at the beginning of this paper, we need to take care, guarding our hearts and minds that we are not changed by the lies of world around us. As such we can take a break from the chore of having to explain or justify our beliefs, and simply rest and revel in the truth God has revealed and called us to live in.

To begin with, let's consider marriage. We live in a society (and again unfortunately for some, in denominations) where attitudes towards marriage cover a range of views—it is an outmoded social convention on its way out; a relationship one engages in for "now" but not "forever"; or some romantic ideal is held up of finding a "soul mate" to whom you never have to say you're sorry. All of this pales in comparison to the glorious vision of marriage presented by Scripture and expounded upon by Luther. Marriage isn't simply some social convention, or legalized means of having sex, but a Divinely ordained vocation, part of God's good and gracious will for us as His children. It is something God is strongly interested in—indeed Luther encourages men and women to pray asking God to bring to them the spouse of His choosing, evoking a sense of trust and expectation for God's will for their life. This relationship men and women are called to is an essential part of God's plan for this world and His kingdom. Knowing this, how could any husband or wife ever wonder or worry if their life matters? But perhaps that's part of the trouble—many in and outside of the church haven't heard and don't know this. Instead, they are depending upon experience or what they have heard in songs, seen in movies or read in novels for their vision and understanding of marriage.

This covenanted relationship is one man and one woman until death do they part.[20] Before we worry about coming up with

---

20. Luther does discuss divorce and how adultery and abandonment can be permissible reasons for divorce. E.g. see "Estate of Marriage" *Luther's Works Vol. 45 The Christian in Society II* p. 30 ff. and "The Sermon on the Mount" *Luther's Works Vol. 21 The Sermon on the Mount and The Magnificat* p. 83 ff.

explanations as to why it isn't two men, two women, or multiple combinations of the sexes, let's enjoy this gift and truth we have been given. Of course there is a time and place for arguments to be made and explanations to be presented—living in a country that allows for the legal arrangement the government calls "same-sex marriage" (which of course in the eyes of God and the Church is an impossibility), we will be called on to give a defense for what we teach and practice. But for sake of ourselves, our families and dare I say our souls, we are best served by directing our attention and energy to growing in our understanding, appreciation and ability to live out these relationships God has blessed us with as spouses, parents and children. Rather than dwell on what is wrong, let's rest in the good we have been given.

If anything needs more work, it is how we regard those in our midst who, for whatever reason, are single. Scripture and Luther are clear there are two states of life blessed by God, marriage and singleness, and in both chastity is expected. As God gives both, they can't be considered contradictory, but rather are complementary and each serves the body of Christ.

The juxtaposition of Luther's writing on children and what we see in society and our churches (officially and unofficially) demonstrates how much things have changed. On one hand I don't think we are to the point where referring to children as a "gift from God" is going to be challenged in our various churches. However, I think it has become the unspoken assumption that while children may be a gift from God, they are a gift we are free to manage, to accept or refuse at our whim.

As mentioned earlier, until the 1930s the Christian church uniformly condemned contraception. Today among Protestants it is not only accepted but also encouraged and among Roman Catholics and Orthodox while officially condemned, many utilize it either openly or in secret. A couple may want to have children, but when they are "ready" financially, emotionally, career-wise etc. (an aside, a couple is never "ready"—having children is an act of faith in the grace and providence of God to provide and nothing less). However, from reading Scripture and Luther, it seems that what makes a couple "ready" is just that—they are married. The most important and necessary step to being ready is already in place: they are husband and wife, in the covenanted relationship of marriage, which is the foundation for the family. To put any other stipulations or conditions in place would seem to indicate a lack of trust in God's will for their life as a couple. I am well aware of all the reasons why a husband and wife might want to delay having children, or limit the size of their family, having heard or spoken many of them. Further, I will concede that some of these reasons may seem to be "good." But might this be a case of settling for what we think is good (a "good" that can be debated) rather than leaving ourselves open to receiving God's best? At this point we should recall that God's best is not always simple and easy nor will it receive unanimous approval by all. I recall my bishop writing an article in our denominational magazine where he praised parenthood, only to be blasted in a letter to the editor in a subsequent issue where he (and the rest of us) were informed that it was perfectly acceptable for Christian couples to forgo children—based solely on the writer's acquaintance with such a couple. So where does our trust lie—our judgment and experience or God? Do we truly want what God wants, or do we want what we want?

Going one step further let's consider briefly the matter of abortion. It was interesting that aside from Luther's acknowledgement in his piece on miscarriage that some women might harm their children either before or after birth, the matter doesn't come up. Given the fact that in many ways he still had the mindset of a Roman Catholic monk, it is safe to conclude Luther thought abortion to be a sin, with no justification. Contrast that with my own denomination, the Evangelical Lutheran Church in Canada, and its statement on the matter: "Stewards of Creation: Respect for Human Life, Evangelical Lutheran Church in Canada

Position on Abortion."[21] This is a nine page document that says in essence "abortion is a regrettable thing, but stuff happens and since we can't judge another's experience we'll go to the fall-back position that God is gracious and forgives." If Luther were to read this he would sue to have his name taken out of the denom-ination's title lest anyone think he was somehow connected with this abomination. One indication of how acceptable abortion has become in our society is that when my wife was expecting our most recent child, on our first visit to the Ob/Gyn we were referred to, the doctor offered the option of aborting given possible complications with the pregnancy. Oddly enough I was standing there in my clericals when she made the offer.[22]

To be sure contraception and abortion are serious issues that deserve more thought, attention and action than they have been given in our churches. But in the spirit of this paper rather than focus on what's wrong, let's consider the good God has given us in children.

It's an indication of where my denomination is at (and perhaps yours as well) that much is being made about the stewardship of creation, the importance of "being green" and appreciating the glory of God in the wonder of creation, yet we hear next to nothing about children—at least not in the way Scripture speaks of them uniformly as a blessing. Luther addressed this in an exchange with a colleague where he expounded on the blessing of children.

> Dr. Justus Jonas praised the glorious blessing which God grants in fruit. "I have a branch with cherries on it hanging over my table," he said, "in order that when I look at it, I may learn the article about divine creation."

---

21. elcic.ca/Public-Policy/documents/AStatementonAbortion.pdf.

22. After Nathaniel had been delivered healthy and happy despite all the medical concerns the same doctor offered to take us on again as patients if we wanted to have another child.

Dr. Martin Luther responded, "Why don't you learn it daily by looking at your children, the fruit of your body? They're there every day, and surely they amount to much more than all the fruit of the trees! There you may see the providence of God, who created them from nothing. In half a year he gave them body, life and limb, and he will also sustain them. Yet we overlook them, as if those gifts of God made us blind and greedy, as it usually happens that men become worse and more greedy when they have offspring; they don't realize that every child is apportioned his lot according to the saying, "The more children the more luck." Dear God, how great are the ignorance and the wickedness of man who doesn't think about the best gift of God but does just the opposite."[23]

If I may expand further, in children we witness the creative capacity and vocation with which God has blessed fathers and mothers, not just in having children but raising them from infancy into adulthood, in essence having a hand in shaping the next generation, the future of the world. While engaged in this task parents have the opportunity to see and experience the grace and providence of God in their lives and the lives of others. If you have doubts about your lack of patience, grace or charity, have kids and discover the depths of your self-centeredness. At the same time, have kids and discover the grace of God (and your children) in forgiving your many shortfalls, and witness the growth of the fruit of the Spirit in your life by God's mercy. Have kids and learn in a whole different way the love God has for His children as you look on your own and marvel that you are loved even more dearly by your heavenly Father. Have children and find yourself faced with scarcity and want in the areas of time, energy and finances to de-

---

23. Martin Luther, "Acknowledging God's Gifts in the Cherry Season," *Luther's Works Vol. 54 Table Talk* (Philadelphia: Fortress Press, 1967), 245.

grees and in ways you could have never imagined, which end up being opportunities to experience the generous providence of God to provide for all we need (not necessarily all we want) in ways and means never imagined.

Children are a gift from God—end of story. As gifts we can't expect, demand nor should we refuse them, but simply be open to receiving them should it be God's will for us. They are the fruit of the marriage relationship, individuals to be loved and celebrated—regardless of what anyone else might think, say or do.

Allow me to conclude with some personal comments. Being in public with our five children, my wife and I have received our fair share of disdainful looks and snarky whispers. Such reactions used to make me angry (and to some extent still do), but lately more often I feel pity, because that could very well have been me had I not blindly stumbled into the grace-filled life God has given me. I wasn't sure about marriage, but in the midst of a six-course load in seminary with no time for anything other than studying I met and married my wife. The thought of children scared me stupid. I was willing to have one, maybe two so they would have company. Through divine guidance and circumstance we have five amazing children and look expectantly to the day when we will meet the child we lost through miscarriage. My hope for my children is that they won't suffer from the same degree of ignorance as did their father. I pray that as they grow up they would learn from what their mother and I teach them intentionally and what they learn from observation, that if God calls them to marriage and parenthood, there is nothing else more important and blessed they could do with their lives. An important part of this will be us holding up to them and ourselves the truths of Scripture and the encouragement of godly men and women like Luther concerning marriage and family.

In conclusion, there is much in this world that would seek to distract and turn us from the gifts God has offered in marriage and family—much that would seek to change us from being and becoming the people God desires. Yet in the midst of these storms, we have been given places of refuge where we can rest and be edified—Scripture, the Confessions, Luther's writings etc. God grant us wisdom to seek out these resources, that through them God would graciously encourage and preserve us, and our families, in the faith, now and unto eternal life.

Pr. Brad Everett, STS, serves Nazareth Lutheran Church in Standard, AB, Ordained in 1998, he received his M.Div. and STM from Lutheran Theological Seminary in Saskatoon. He is Dean of the Rocky Mountain Chapter of the Society of the Holy Trinity (STS). He and his wife Manny are parents to five wonderful children.

Epilogue

The Lake Louise Commission participants gathered to address the debacle and disaster in two of the Lutheran Churches in North America as they forsake their Godly heritage of Scripture, Tradition, and the Confessions for a mess of potage prepared by the *zeitgeist*. The members listened to the voice of Martin Luther speaking through the centuries about the first order of creation, the Sacred Family, and effectively addressed the main issues of the day.

This distinguished Father in the faith, Doctor Luther, always spoke clearly and effectively about the three orders of creation: the State, the Church, and the First order of creation, the Sacred Family. Though they are separate orders with clearly defined areas of responsibility, they share a unity in their various responsibilities and in their own mandates, to fill the earth and subdue it and have dominion over all the creatures of the earth. They were to do so in obedience to the Lord, honouring his will, his way, his word, his design, and the image of God in which human kind was created, male and female, husband and wife, co-creators with God.

The State has the responsibility to honour and protect the family, permitting it to rear their children in the fear and love of the Lord, and indeed fill the earth and subdue it. The State is to rule with the authority given by God, under the supervision of the Law: the law both engraved on our hearts and the law later given by revelation.

The Church, in its visible form, has the responsibility to honour and protect the family, so that its members can hear and live under

God's gracious moral law embedded in the Ten Commandments; and most important, to hear and live under the call of the Gospel, becoming new creatures in Christ, rightly distinguishing between the Law and the Gospel.

Both Church and State, each operating in its own clearly defined area, have the responsibility to honour and protect the family within God's design and intention. The very well-being of the Church and State are themselves very much affected and influenced by the well-being of the family they themselves have been charged to honour and protect within their own spheres.

God's design for human kind, in all three orders of creation, is as beautiful and magnificent and holy as is God's design for creation and the universe as we see it. God knows what He is doing.

But sin and evil still poison our world, and when we depart from God's intentions and design, sin and evil are given the opportunity to wreck much greater havoc in all three orders, and they do.

In many countries of the West, the State has already decided that God's design for the family, Husband and Wife, is outdated and inadequate. God does not know what God is doing, and with our knowledge we can improve on God's good creation. So also have many denominations essentially declared the Scripture to be outdated and inadequate and proceeded to redefine the essence of the family, replacing the good news of repentance and forgiveness with the gospel of inclusion, dividing the visible church, and scattering the flock.

We now live in a world filled with error in its view of the first order of creation. Indeed, for some, there is no such thing as a first order of creation. But we also live in a world which is beginning to experience the consequences of the demolition of the first order of creation. Luther would also have described our world in both the church and family as "wretched deprivation."

Our beloved Father in the faith had the courage to stand up and speak the truth concerning all three orders in creation. We must find the courage to do the same. We must find the courage to call all our brothers and sisters, whether they are prepared to listen or not, to hearken to the Word of the Lord. If we say nothing, we only encourage the disasters that are on the way, and become accountable ourselves. We have no choice but to let the clear word of brother Martin Luther, grounded in Scripture and the tradition of the Church, be heard in our time, too.

Acknowledgements

This project, like the others, the Banff and Jasper Commissions, has been made possible through the efforts, talents and resources of many people. We say thank you to the congregation at Ascension Lutheran in Calgary whose vision and support made it possible, and who authorized their pastor, K. Glen Johnson, to devote the time necessary to manage and oversee the project.

We say thank you to the many people who contributed the finances and other resources necessary for the Lake Louise Commission.

We say thank you to all those present at the meeting of the Commission in Banff, March 27–29, 2011; first to all those who presented the papers included in this volume, and also to Doug Gust, the chairman of the congregation, and his wife Edana, and Manny Everett.

We say thank you to The American Lutheran Publicity Bureau for agreeing to publish the papers from the Lake Louise Commission and to Frederick J. Schumacher, ALPB Executive Director, for championing this volume, and selecting and providing a very fitting cover.

We say thank you to Martin A. Christiansen whose exemplary work of formatting and design have brought this and the two other volumes to completion. And we say thank you also to Dorothy Zelenko of the ALPB and Pastor Bradley Everett for their careful editing work.

And finally we say thank you to God in whose power all things are made possible!

Made in the USA
Charleston, SC
23 November 2011